WOMEN & MUTUAL FUNDS

WOMEN & MUTUAL FUNDS
Gain Understanding and Be in Control

DONALD S. GUDHUS, MBA

iUniverse, Inc.
New York Bloomington Shanghai

WOMEN & MUTUAL FUNDS
Gain Understanding and Be in Control

iUniverse books may be ordered through booksellers or by contacting:

iUniverse
1663 Liberty Drive
Bloomington, IN 47403
www.iuniverse.com
1-800-Authors (1-800-288-4677)

Because of the dynamic nature of the Internet, any Web addresses or links contained in this book may have changed since publication and may no longer be valid.

The information, ideas, and suggestions in this book are not intended to render professional advice. Before following any suggestions contained in this book, you should consult your personal accountant or other financial advisor. Neither the author nor the publisher shall be liable or responsible for any loss or damage allegedly arising as a consequence of your use or application of any information or suggestions in this book.

ISBN: 978-0-595-45703-8 (pbk)
ISBN: 978-0-595-90004-6 (ebk)

Printed in the United States of America

For Mom & Dad

Contents

Acknowledgments ix

Introduction xi

Chapter 1: Types of Mutual Funds and Related Information 1

  Stock Mutual Funds 1

  Bond Mutual Funds 2

  Types of Mutual Funds 3

  Benefits of Mutual Funds 5

  Mutual Fund Annual Expenses 6

Chapter 2: Selecting Mutual Funds 8

  Qualitative Measures 9

  Statistical Factors 10

   Percentile Rank in Category/Mean (Percent Return) *11*

   Tenure *14*

   Standard Deviation and Beta *14*

   Alpha *16*

   Sharpe Ratio *17*

   Fund Fees, Expenses, and Other *17*

  Which Mutual Fund to Choose? 20

  Summary 20

Chapter 3: Asset Allocation 22

  A Comparative Example of the Asset Allocation Process in Action 23

  Importance of Asset Allocation 23

Quantitative Impact of Asset Allocation 24

Other Reasons for Asset Allocation. 25

Advantages and Disadvantages of Asset Allocation 26

Risk Profile Questionnaire 26

Summary 28

Chapter 4: Portfolio Construction **31**

Portfolio Construction Assumptions. 32

Initial Asset Allocation 34

Quantifying Your Initial Allocation 35

Illustrating the Adjustment Process. 36

Summary 39

Chapter 5: Monitoring and Rebalancing or Reallocating **41**

Monitoring. 42

Rebalancing 42

Reallocating 45

Summary 45

Chapter 6: The Mutual Fund Investment Process—A Review **47**

Chapter 7: Conclusion **49**

About the Author **51**

Financial Glossary **53**

References **67**

Index **69**

Acknowledgments

Many people provided incredible support for this undertaking. Special thanks go to my niece, Lynn. A gifted writer and teacher, her insights into and observations about publishing were invaluable. My sister-in-law, Judy, showed her talent for questioning. The result is a book that conveys information in a simple and understandable way. To my brother, Den, I cannot sufficiently convey my appreciation for his relentless enthusiasm for this project and tactful commentary. And to my nephew, Keith, for his continued support of this project.

Words cannot express my gratitude to several friends. Scott Black, founder and president of Delphi Management in Boston, portfolio manager of the Delphi Value Fund, and a member of *Barron's* Roundtable. He provided succinct commentary and very useful suggestions. Eleanor Betz, Esq., imparted advice in areas where women would require greater emphasis. John Izenour, who directs graphic design at Venturi, Scott Brown and Associates, an architectural firm in Philadelphia, provided computer and graphics expertise. Ron Rizzuto, finance professor at the University of Denver, provided that special academic insight, particularly in the statistical discussion. Maria Walker, former special assistant to the late Thomas Foglietta, a former Pennsylvania congressman, presented incisive observations on overall tone and writing style. Carol Walsh offered feedback that coaxed me to simplify certain points that otherwise would have remained overlooked and overly complex.

Finally, I want to thank my investment clients. Their trust and confidence in my methodology for mutual fund investing encouraged me to share it with others so they, too, could benefit.

To all, my heartfelt thanks.

Introduction

○ ○

Without goals, and plans to reach them, you are like a ship that has set sail with no destination.

—Fitzhugh Dodson, PhD
Noted expert on parenting

Since 1924, when the first mutual fund was offered to the investing public, their numbers have swelled to over seventeen thousand. Total mutual fund value exceeds $7.5 trillion. Not only have the offerings proliferated, but they have become increasingly complex. Accompanying this enormous increase in the number and complexity of mutual fund offerings has been a huge increase in anxiety among investors. This is because some fundamental questions have not been adequately answered. When synthesized, these questions boil down to:

1. What is a mutual fund?

2. How do I choose those mutual funds that are best for me?

In the following pages, answers are provided to those questions, along with a lot more practical information. *Women & Mutual Funds: Gain Understanding and Be in Control*, takes you from understanding what a mutual fund is and selecting mutual funds that are suitable for you through creating a portfolio of mutual funds and suggestions about monitoring and adjusting that portfolio when necessary.

But why do you need to know this? Willingly or unwillingly, many of us are participants in this industry. This can happen in a number of ways, including:

- Through your employer you may participate in your company's 401(k), 403(b), simplified employee pension (SEP) plan, or other retirement plan.

- To augment your company's retirement plan, you may contribute to a traditional individual retirement account (IRA) or a Roth IRA.

- You may be starting a business and have decided to transfer your former company-sponsored 401(k) to a rollover IRA.

- You're in business for yourself and have decided to contribute to a savings incentive match plan for employees of small employers (SIMPLE) IRA.

- You may be saving for your children's education by using a Section 529 college savings plan.

- You may simply have an individual account with one or more mutual fund companies.

The list goes on. There are many ways in which you may become an owner of mutual funds.

You owe it to yourself and your family to become more knowledgeable about mutual funds. It's in your best interest to gain a better understanding. It's your money. Your family depends on you. The future is up to you. A great place to begin learning more about mutual funds is by reading this book.

WHAT IS A MUTUAL FUND?

A mutual fund is defined as an open-end investment company that invests money of its shareholders in a diversified group of securities of other corporations.[1] These securities are typically common stocks or government, agency, or corporate bonds. Confused? Let's try again. It's a holding device, or even better, an investment vehicle, that primarily contains an assortment of corporate stocks and bonds issued by corporations and federal, state, or local governments or their agencies (i.e., Fannie Mae). To say it another way: A mutual fund is like a grocery store. The grocery store is the investment vehicle or holder of various foods. These foods represent the stocks or bonds of companies and organizations that include the federal government, as well as state and local governments. As with all investments, an investment in a mutual fund is not insured or guaranteed by the Federal Deposit Insurance Corporation (FDIC) or any other government agency. It is possible to lose money by investing in a mutual fund.

WHY SHOULD YOU PARTICIPATE IN THE EQUITY MARKET?

Equity, generally known as common stock, is defined as a security that represents ownership in a corporation.

---

1. *Webster's Third New International Dictionary, Unabridged.* Springfield, MA: Merriam-Webster, Inc., 1993. All future references to Webster's are to this edition.

The fundamental reason for participating in the equity market is that it offers an opportunity to share in the growth of the U.S. economy or even the global economy. By participating, you give yourself the opportunity to achieve returns that historically have been appreciably higher than bonds and certificates of deposit and significantly greater than the rate of inflation.

The benefits include the possibility of retiring more comfortably or accelerating the purchase of a vacation home. Based on the returns from the past thirty years, equity investing makes such goals more doable; conversely, such goals would be more difficult to attain, if not impossible, using alternative investments. Additionally, entry into equity investing using mutual funds is easy. It doesn't take thousands of dollars to start.

The table that follows compares the annualized returns from large company stocks (represented by the Standard & Poor's 500-stock index with dividends reinvested); small company stocks (represented by: [a] 1976–81—the New York Stock Exchange (NYSE) fifth quintile returns; [b] 1982– March 2001—Dimensional Fund Advisors Small Company portfolio; and [c] April 2001– 05—Dimensional Fund Advisors U.S. Micro Cap fund); long-term corporate bonds (represented by Salomon Brothers Long-Term High-Grade Corporate Bond Index [approximate maturity twenty years]); long-term government bonds (represented by one-bond portfolio [approximate maturity twenty years]); intermediate-term government bonds (represented by one-bond portfolio [approximate maturity five years]); U.S. treasury bills (represented by one-bond portfolio [approximate maturity thirty days]); and inflation (represented by the U.S. consumer price index, not seasonally adjusted).

	Large Company	Small Company	Long-Term Corporate Bonds	Long-Term Government Bonds	Intermediate-Term Gov't Bonds	U.S. Treasury Bills	CPI
1976–1980	13.95%	37.35%	2.36%	1.68%	5.08%	7.77%	9.21%
1980–1985	14.71	18.82	17.86	16.83	15.80	10.30	4.85
1986–1990	13.14	0.58	10.43	10.75	9.34	6.83	4.13
1991–1995	16.57	24.51	12.22	13.10	8.81	4.29	2.79
1996–2000	18.35	10.87	5.79	7.49	6.17	5.18	2.54
2001–2005	0.54	16.44	9.30	7.72	5.22	2.13	2.49

Source: Data and categories were provided by Ibbotson, Roger G. *Stocks, Bonds, Bills and Inflation, Valuation Edition, 2006 Yearbook.* Chicago.

With a few exceptions, returns from large-company and small-company stocks exceeded the returns from bonds and treasury bills. When compared to inflation, the returns from large companies and small companies provided greater purchasing power protection. But it should be remembered that large-company and small-company investments are riskier than investments in bonds or treasury bills.

What does this mean in terms of dollars and cents? OK, let's say on January 2, 1976, you invested $1,000 in each of the categories. The resulting values of these investments on December 30, 2005, (after thirty years) are:

	Value	Annualized Returns
Large Company	$36,335	12.72%
Small Company	$127,876	17.55%
Long-Term Corporate Bonds	$15,434	9.55%
Long-Term Government Bonds	$15,161	9.49%
Intermediate-Term Government Bonds	$11,063	8.34%
U.S. Treasury Bills	$5,827	6.05%

The above table shows the following:

1. The returns earned from the investment in the small-company category were 8.3 to 21.9 times greater than the returns from bonds and treasury bills.

2. The returns from the investment in the large-company category were 2.3 to 6.2 times greater than the returns from bonds and treasury bills.

Compelling support for investing in stocks? Absolutely!

MY STORY

Upon earning my MBA in financial management, I started my climb up the proverbial corporate ladder. I progressively gained a solid grounding in corporate finance at such companies as Coca-Cola International, RCA-Hertz Corporation, and Conrail. It was during this climb that a variety of personal financial issues began to surface. And I had no answers. These issues included insurance, selecting the right investments for my IRAs, 401(k)s, and other kinds of accounts, as well as managing my cash.

To my chagrin, there was no single source I could rely on to provide objective guidance in these and other financial areas. Not being able to go to one source for personal financial guidance astonished me. This thought festered for some time.

The more I investigated and analyzed these areas, the more interested I became. Realizing that there had to be many people out there like me, I pondered the possibility of a career change. Then I decided to do it. I went back to school and completed the coursework in personal financial planning and completed the CFP® Professional Education Program from the College for Financial Planning.

This expertise, along with my personal experiences and solid financial background, established the foundation for a new business model. In 1993, I started Oracle Financial Group. From the beginning, it became apparent that many people needed this type of financial advice.

However, as human nature would have it, a majority of people in need of assistance never think of searching for it. I wanted to do something about that, so others could avoid the financial pitfalls I had encountered.

It took me more than ten years to write this book because it took that long to gain the necessary real-life experience and to fully develop the methodology to provide a road map that could be used to select mutual funds and construct, manage, and monitor a mutual fund portfolio.

But why did I write this book for women? There are a number of reasons. First, a significant number of my clients are women. I have found that women tend to be very focused when it comes to new material and quickly move up the learning curve. Furthermore, not only am I a personal financial advisor, but I am a teacher, too. As a personal financial advisor, I have a responsibility to question preconceived notions and to correct those notions when necessary.

Also, women, particularly in the area of investments, have been significantly underserved. However, women increasingly handle financial matters for their households. They should be afforded the tools that can improve their financial skills.

WHAT TYPE OF WOMEN WOULD BENEFIT MOST FROM READING THIS BOOK?

This book is for all women, regardless of career or stage of life. It will benefit full-time or part-time professional women; stay-at-home moms; divorcées; widows; pre-retirees; and retired women. *Women & Mutual Funds: Gain Understanding and Be in Control* is a quick read that simplifies a complex subject. It provides a platform to gain knowledge and understanding about mutual funds and the effort it takes to construct and maintain a portfolio.

There are a number of books in the marketplace on mutual funds. There are books that concentrate on just one or two aspects of mutual funds. Other books spotlight their list of the "best" mutual funds. Some books go through a lengthy diatribe on everything you ever wanted to know about mutual funds. And somewhere in the midst of those hundreds of pages the reader may become lost, confused, and frustrated.

My book is different. First, as you can see, it's short. Second, it's the only book on mutual funds solely devoted to the development and maintenance of a portfolio of mutual funds. All the noise has been removed. It doesn't recommend mutual funds. It doesn't use a cookie-cutter approach. It does take you on a step-by-step expedition that starts by describing the kinds of mutual funds that are available in the marketplace. This sets the stage for a discussion of the overall portfolio construction process. This process begins with the factors that should be considered when selecting mutual funds.

The next chapter provides an overview of investing among various categories and styles of mutual funds and why allocating your investment dollars among different categories and styles of mutual funds is so important. This is called asset allocation. It presents a comparative example of the asset allocation process in action and continues with a discussion of the importance of asset allocation. It concludes by introducing a tool to gauge your tolerance for risk, known as the Risk Profile Questionnaire.

The book goes on to show how a portfolio is constructed. This includes a way of initially allocating your investment dollars and a method to adjust that allocation in the attempt to reach expected results, still maintaining comparable risk and rate of return standards achieved in the past. This is called "historic risk" and "historic rate of return."

Following this is a discussion on the need to monitor and rebalance or reallocate your portfolio. These are the techniques that help provide the assurance that your portfolio remains consistent with your goals and needs. The failure to regularly evaluate your portfolio is like trying to make a cell phone call, knowing you didn't recharge the phone or that you're making the call in a dead zone. In both instances, you know the outcome is not going to be favorable. That is, you're not going to be able to make the call!

Even if you decide not to spend the time and energy to develop and manage your portfolio, the book provides a wealth of information. You can use this information as a basis for questioning your financial advisor. Essentially, it levels the playing field. And finally, it can offer you the kind of control of your investments that you probably thought you would never have.

As mentioned earlier, *Women & Mutual Funds* is a quick read. It simplifies a rather complex subject. So begin the journey and enjoy the ride. I hope you'll find the book interesting. And remember, it's your money. I hope this book inspires you to action.

Chapter 1:

Types of Mutual Funds and Related Information

There is quite an array of mutual funds in the marketplace. They range from the very conservative money market fund, to various types of bond funds, to all kinds of stock funds that include the high-risk sector funds, such as technology and biotechnology.

STOCK MUTUAL FUNDS

These are funds whose holdings are usually dominated by the common stock of various companies. A common stock is a security that represents ownership in a corporation. When delineated according to investment style, stock mutual funds are classified as: value, growth, or blend. They can be further divided between domestic (U.S.) and international funds. They can be further grouped according to the size of companies owned. This is called "category." There are three categories of companies: large capitalization ("cap") or company, mid-cap, and small cap.

There are three basic stock mutual fund investment styles:

Value
: Typically contains holdings that have lower price to earnings and price to book value ratios in relation to growth funds. [The calculation of a company's price to earnings ratio is: market price per share/earnings per share.] Fund holdings may include companies that are not followed by the overall market and companies that are in turnaround situations (referred to as out-of-favor companies). Their holdings are generally reasonably priced and yet show characteristics of performance improvement.

Growth
: Usually contains holdings that have higher price to earnings and price to book value ratios in relation to value funds. Fund holdings generally exhibit or are expected to exhibit accelerating earnings and market share growth (referred to as companies that are "in favor"). Such funds pursue capital appreciation; current income is either not considered or is a secondary issue.

Blend
: Includes a combination of value and growth companies. In this category there are large cap, mid-cap, small cap, and international funds.

The market value or capitalization of a company is determined by multiplying the number of common shares of stock outstanding by the market price of a share of stock. Mutual funds are classified according to capitalization and fall into three categories:

Large Cap
: Funds that hold a majority of companies that each have a capitalization of generally over $10 billion.

Mid-Cap
: Funds that hold a majority of companies that each have a capitalization generally between $2 billion and $10 billion.

Small Cap
: Funds that hold a majority of companies that each have a capitalization of under $2 billion.

BOND MUTUAL FUNDS

These are funds whose primary (and possibly exclusive) holdings are in the debt securities of the U.S. government, its agencies, municipalities, or corporations, or foreign governments. A bond is an IOU, a promise by the borrower to repay the lender on a certain date in the future the amount that was borrowed. During the life of the bond, the borrower promises to pay the lender a specific amount of interest, periodically (usually semiannually) for the use of the money.

Bond funds are delineated based on style and credit worthiness of their holdings. Style means the average life or duration of the bonds in the portfolio: short, intermediate, and long. The longer the average life or duration of bond holdings, the greater the bond fund's sensitivity to interest rate changes. (As interest rates rise, the underlying value of the bond holdings drops. Conversely, as interest rates drop, the underlying value of the bond holdings rise.)

Credit quality indicates how secure the companies are that have issued the bonds. They are broadly defined as: high (most secure), medium, and low. There is a further breakdown of credit rating: U.S. government/agency has the highest overall credit rating and is the most secure; next is AAA, the highest credit rating for corporate bond issuers; and proceeding to holdings that are not rated and are considered the riskiest.

TYPES OF MUTUAL FUNDS

There are as many types of mutual funds in the marketplace as there are reasons or needs or desires for investing. Below is a general categorization of the variety of mutual funds available:

Money Market Funds	Contain short-term, high-quality securities that mainly provide safety of principal; the fund's current income is a secondary consideration (includes tax-free funds).
Short/Intermediate Bonds	Contain a mixture of U.S. government securities and credit-worthy corporate bonds that usually have an effective maturity and average duration or portfolio life typically between one to ten years.
Long-Term Bonds	Contain a variety of corporate bonds that emphasize credit-worthy companies and usually have an effective maturity greater than ten years (average duration or portfolio life could be less than ten years).
High-Yield Bonds	Include a range of higher yielding, lower rated corporate bonds (can include tax-free funds).
Municipal Bonds	Typically contain holdings of local governments and political subdivisions within a specific state (can be federal, state, and local tax free).

Balanced Funds	Contain a mixture of common stocks and corporate and U.S. government bonds. These funds stress both current income and capital appreciation. The equity portion of this type of fund is generally in the large cap category and typically represents the majority of holdings.
Value Funds	Typically contain holdings that have lower price to earnings and price to book value ratios in relation to growth funds. [The calculation of a company's price to earnings ratio is: market price per share divided by earnings per share.] Fund holdings may include companies that are not followed by the overall market and companies that are in turnaround situations. Their holdings are generally priced more reasonably and yet show characteristics of performance improvement. In this category there are large cap, mid-cap, small cap, and international funds.
Growth Funds	Usually contain holdings that possess higher price to earnings and price to book value ratios in relation to value funds. Fund holdings generally exhibit or are expected to exhibit accelerated earnings and market share growth. Such funds pursue capital appreciation; current income is either not considered or is a secondary issue. In this category there are also large cap, mid-cap, small cap, and international funds.
Blend Funds	Include a combination of value and growth companies. In this category there are large cap, mid-cap, small cap, and international funds.
Sector/Country Funds	Include companies within the same industry or country; for example, energy, technology, biotechnology, China, Japan, Russia.
Domestic Funds	Include companies that are primarily in the United States.
International Funds	Include companies that are in diverse markets and almost exclusively outside the United States.
Global Funds	Include companies in diverse markets but can have significant holdings in U.S. companies.

Exchange Traded Funds

Commonly referred to as ETFs, these are a collection of common stocks or bonds that mirror the performance of a market index. ETFs cover all asset classes, such as U.S. large companies, small companies, overseas companies, etc. Unlike an index mutual fund, these funds can be purchased or sold throughout the trading day. The stocks or bonds that make up the ETF do not change, regardless of how they're performing.

Index Mutual Funds

A collection of common stocks that mirrors the performance of a market index, that is, S&P 500. There are a limited number of indexes covered. Unlike the ETF, index funds can only be purchased or sold after the close of the trading day. The stocks or bonds that make up the index do not change regardless of how they're performing.

BENEFITS OF MUTUAL FUNDS

The benefits of owning mutual funds are unique and are very different from owning individual stocks or bonds. These benefits range from offering immediate diversification to only requiring a small amount of money to purchase shares. Here are some of the benefits.

- **Offer diversification.** Mutual funds are typically comprised of a number of securities that cover a wide range of business sectors and industries. These areas could include technology and communications, consumer, business and financial services, and consumer goods, industrial material, energy, and utilities. Such an array can help to spread risk and potentially reduce the impact of market fluctuations.

- **Afford the ability to allocate assets.** Most mutual funds focus on different categories and styles of investing. By combining several of these, you can develop a mixture of funds that could include stocks and bonds of large organizations, midsize companies, small companies, and overseas companies, as well as funds that focus on a sector of the economy or a particular country. You get to decide the allocation. There are also styles of investing to consider. That is, there are mutual funds with a growth orientation or value orientation as well as funds that invest in a combination of growth and value—a blend orientation.

- **Provide professional management.** When you purchase shares in a mutual fund you engage the services of a professional money manager or a team of money managers. They execute the day-to-day investment decisions that are consistent with the fund's objectives as articulated in the fund's prospectus.

- **Small transaction cost.** The cost is dependant on whether you purchase a "load" fund or a "no load" fund. Typically, with a Class A share load fund, there is an upfront sales charge of approximately 4.75 percent to 5.75 percent. With B and C shares there is no upfront sales charge, but there is a deferred sales charge. With B shares, this deferred sales charge declines over several years and usually begins at around 5 percent to 6 percent. With C shares, there is typically a 1 percent deferred charge that lasts for one year. On the other hand, with "no load" funds there is no upfront or deferred sales charge.

- **Relatively small amount of money needed to purchase shares.** Some funds allow purchases with as little as $25. This is unlike the purchase of individual common stocks or bonds for which (transaction) cost-effective purchases typically cost more.

MUTUAL FUND ANNUAL EXPENSES

Mutual funds that are sold through financial intermediaries, i.e., banks, brokerages, insurance companies, etc., typically come in three share types—A shares, B shares, and C shares. This table summarizes the typical expenses incurred by an investor when purchasing either A shares, B shares, or C shares.

Types of Expense/Type of Shares	A	B	C
Sales Charge	Front-End Charge Typically 4.75%–5.75%	No Front-End Charge	No Front-End Charge
Contingent Deferred Sales Charge*	No	Yes, generally 6 years. Converts to A shares	Yes, generally 1 year. Does not convert to A shares
Management Fee**	All share types are the same. See Below.		
Rule 12(b)-1 Fee***	Generally up to .25%	Generally up to .75% more than A shares	Generally up to .75% more than A shares

The expenses for the above noted share classes are typical for stock "load mutual funds." Expenses for stock "no load funds," while not shown, are similar to A shares, but without the front-end sales charge and possibly no 12(b)-1 fee.

* A contingent deferred sales charge is a fee imposed by a mutual fund company for the premature redemption of a portion or all of an account from the mutual fund family.

** Management fee is the portfolio manager's fee to manage the investments. Generally, for a stock mutual fund it ranges between 0.75 percent to 2.00 percent, depending on the category and style of the mutual fund.

*** Rule 12(b)-1 fee covers distribution costs of the mutual fund. It includes fees paid for marketing and selling shares, and advertising, printing and mailing costs associated with prospectuses and sales literature. This fee is more commonly charged by "load mutual funds."

Chapter 2:

Selecting Mutual Funds

○ ○

The real risk lies in continuing to do things the way they've always been done.

—Muriel Siebert
First woman to own a seat on the
New York Stock Exchange

Beginning with this chapter and through the remainder of the book, the discussion will be devoted to stock mutual funds. There will be no further discussion of bond mutual funds.

Now, before you begin this chapter, I want to let you know that there are some difficult parts. But don't get frustrated or discouraged. The important thing is that you understand the concept that underlies each factor and develop an appreciation for what the data suggests.

Deciding on which mutual funds to invest in is not simply a matter of some mystical force guiding your hand over a newspaper listing, and voilà, giving you your selections. Choosing is not easy; it's hard work.

To make the task manageable, use a process that is easy to understand and offers a logical sequence. The number of mutual funds you should analyze is based on the type of account you wish to have, for example, individual or regular account or IRA or company-sponsored retirement account (usually a 401(k) or 403(b) and the category and style of mutual funds that you want to select, such as a fund with a large cap value, small cap growth, and so on. Typically, your company-sponsored retirement plan will only have a few selections within any category and style of mutual funds. This differs from an IRA or regular account, for which the number of possible mutual funds can range from a few hundred to a few thousand. Qualitative measures and statistical factors should be used to provide the kind of information that allows you to progressively cull the available funds so that you end up with the most appropriate selections for you.

Whether it's an individual or regular account or IRA or company-sponsored retirement account, following a process that guides your selection will provide the best results. The process I encourage you to follow is broken down into two major components: qualitative measures and statistical factors. While both major components are addressed, significant emphasis is placed on the statistical factors.

To obtain the actual data used in the process, I recommend you use the Morningstar™ Mutual Fund reports. To record the statistical information, you should use the worksheet that immediately precedes the Morningstar report on the following pages. When completed for all the mutual funds you wish to analyze in a certain category and style, the worksheet will hold the information you need to make your selection.

Several worksheets may be necessary. Each worksheet should be for a different category and style of mutual fund, such as large cap value, mid-cap growth, and so forth. To illustrate this process, the Morningstar report◆ for the Baron Partners Fund is used. This is a mid-cap growth fund. The Morningstar report has been alphabetically notated (A–K) to quickly identify those measures and statistics that are discussed. (These Morningstar reports are generally available at your local library.)

QUALITATIVE MEASURES

Before you begin with the statistical component of the process, you should pause and think about why you wish to invest. Your selection process should start by defining your goals or reasons for your investment. For example:

- Are you saving for retirement?
- Are you retired and seeking maximum income from your investment portfolio?
- Are you saving to make a significant purchase in the future?

Your goals or reasons for the investment will help you establish parameters. These include the amount of time you'll have before the money is needed. Also, you should decide on the level of risk you might be willing to accept to achieve the desired level of funds to attain your goals. Your responses to the Risk Profile Questionnaire in the next chapter on asset allocation will help define your risk tolerance.

Another issue to examine is the kind of account you wish to establish. This will often dictate the time you'll need to develop a portfolio. For example:

- Is the investment a rollover from a 401(k) or 403(b)? In this instance, you may need the complete portfolio to be constructed.

- Is this an individual account that will focus on tax efficiency? As noted above, this may require a totally new portfolio to be developed.

- Is it an IRA that will be used to complement your active 401(k) or 403(b)? A workplace retirement plan typically offers a limited number of categories and styles of funds from which to choose so you may be in search of funds to close gaps in your workplace plan. Those gaps may include a large cap value, a mid-cap growth, a small cap value, or an international fund.

A third measure to assess is the degree to which your interests are protected. Morningstar's Stewardship Grade provides an overall assessment of the manner in which the mutual fund is run; the degree to which the interests of management, the board of directors, and investors are aligned; and the protection of shareholder interests from potentially conflicting management interests. Refer to "A" in the Morningstar report. Baron Partners Fund has a rating of C. On a scale of A–F, that excludes E, this rating is considered average.

Once you have completed the qualitative component of the process, you're ready to begin with the statistical factors. Don't stop now! You can do it! You are now on your way to realizing your goals. However, a note of caution is appropriate: Historical information is used to help you determine your portfolio, but it is important to know that a fund's past performance does not guarantee its future performance. That being said, history still remains an excellent guide to the future, when properly used.

STATISTICAL FACTORS

I have tested many statistics to find ones that proved to be the most beneficial in assisting me in the selection of mutual funds. This testing has resulted in the following statistical factors: percentile rank in category/mean (percent return); tenure; standard deviation and beta; alpha; Sharpe ratio; and fund fees and expenses. When these factors were used collectively, they provided the best guide for selecting mutual funds.

Percentile Rank in Category/Mean (Percent Return)

This is the first statistical factor I recommend for consideration. **Percentile rank in category/mean** is a measure that shows a mutual fund's rank, in terms of total return (percentile). It shows how a fund performed in relation to all the mutual funds in a particular category and style of investing. To view it from a different perspective, it would be the equivalent of a student's class ranking and grade point average within his or her academic major.

This factor is important because the fund's rank is the result of a myriad of variables that have influenced it over a period of time, such as one, three, five, or ten years. The lower the number, the better the fund ranks in its class. So, for example, a rank of five is better than ten, and a rank of one is better than five.

But what are some of the variables that could influence a fund's rank? These variables may include but are not limited to the portfolio manager's stock selection ability, the risks taken by the fund manager to achieve the returns, fund expenses, portfolio turnover, the state of the economy, earnings from the companies held in the fund, inflation, interest rates, and the political landscape.

Refer to "B" in the Morningstar report. This factor is reported in four places. Baron Partners Fund was in the second percentile for all funds in this category and style and attained a return of 21.6 percent for one year. Only ten funds in the same category and style—mid-cap growth—performed better than Baron Partners for the one-year period. Alternatively, over one thousand funds in this category and style performed below Baron Partners for the one-year period.

For the three-year, five-year, and ten-year periods, it ranked in the first, first, and fourth percentiles and returned 25.5 percent, 16.8 percent, and 15.3 percent, respectively. (Please note that the benchmark index is the Russell Mid-Cap Growth Index.) The worksheet has been populated with these statistics as well as the other statistics.

Time period is a very important consideration when trying to assess percentile rank in category. While ten years should be considered, many funds may not have such a life span. How many years should you realistically analyze? This brings us to the next factor and one that drives the time period to be analyzed—tenure of the portfolio manager.

Statistical Analysis Worksheet
Mutual Fund Category Mid-Cap
Mutual Fund Style Growth

Statistical Factors Fund Name(s)	Percent Rank in Category/Mean			Portfolio Manager's Tenure	Measures of Risk					Fund Fees & Expenses				
	3 Years	5 Years	10 Years		Standard Deviation	Beta	R-Squared	Alpha	Sharpe	Expense Ratio	12(b)-1	Turnover Ratio	Front-End Load	Deferred Load/
Baron Partners	1 / 25.5%	1 / 16.8%	4 / 15.3%	15	13.28	1.02	73	9.00	1.54	1.45%	0.25%	38%	0.00%	0.00%

Data through December 31, 2006. Reprinted by permission of Morningstar.

Baron Partners

	Ticker	Load	NAV	Yield	(K) Total Assets	Mstar Category
	BPTRX	None	$22.34	0.0%	$2,302 mil	Mid-Cap Growth

Governance and Management

(A) **Stewardship Grade:** C

(C) **Portfolio Manager(s)**

Ron Baron has been at the helm since the fund's 1992 inception, and given that he owns the advisor, he should be here for a long time. His firm employs roughly 18 analysts and portfolio managers, but he's the driving force behind this fund's portfolio.

Strategy

Manager Ron Baron buys companies he thinks can double in price over the next four years, focusing on rapidly growing firms trading at prices that don't yet reflect their potential. His dislike of short product cycles keeps the fund out of the technology sector. This fund, a partnership until it was converted to a mutual fund in 2003, can also short stocks and use leverage. Typically, individual short positions are quite small. The fund uses leverage (borrows money) to amplify its equity exposure when the manager is bullish on stocks, up to a maximum of one third of its assets including leverage.

Performance 12-31-06

	1st Qtr	2nd Qtr	3rd Qtr	4th Qtr	Total
2002	4.05	-7.40	-22.04	8.63	-18.40
2003	-8.34	19.93	6.14	15.49	34.76
2004	12.89	4.11	2.32	18.58	42.35
2005	-0.74	5.39	2.97	6.17	14.37
2006	12.81	-2.65	1.14	9.43	21.55

Trailing (B)	Total Return%	+/- S&P 500	+/- Russ MG	%Rank (B) Cat	Growth of $10,000
3 Mo	9.43	2.73	2.48	11	10,943
6 Mo	10.68	-2.06	2.76	11	11,068
1 Yr	21.55	5.76	10.89	2	12,155
3 Yr Avg	25.54	15.10	12.81	1	19,385
5 Yr Avg	16.82	10.63	8.80	1	21,756
10 Yr Avg	15.33	6.91	6.71	4	41,632
15 Yr Avg	—	—	—		—

Tax Analysis	Tax-Adj Rtn%	%Rank Cat	Tax-Cost Rat	%Rank Cat
3 Yr (estimated)	24.92	1	0.49	25
5 Yr (estimated)	16.11	1	0.61	43
10 Yr (estimated)	14.98	3	0.30	6

Potential Capital Gain Exposure: 27% of assets (J)

Historical Profile

Return	High
Risk	High
Rating	★★★★ Above Avg

Investment Style: Equity Stock %
95% 83% 90% 99%

▼ Manager Change
▽ Partial Manager Change

Growth of $10,000
— Investment Values of Fund
— Investment Values of S&P 500

64.6
48.4
33.6
24.8
17.0
10.8

Performance Quartile (within Category)

	1995	1996	1997	1998	1999	2000	2001	2002	2003	2004	2005	12-06	History
NAV	5.39	6.45	10.44	11.62	14.07	14.70	12.34	10.07	12.17	16.85	18.43	22.34	NAV
Total Return % (B)	45.68	19.67	61.86	11.30	21.06	4.48	-16.05	-18.40	34.76	42.35	14.37	21.55	Total Return % (B)
+/-S&P 500	8.10	-3.29	29.50	-17.28	0.04	13.58	-4.16	3.70	6.08	31.47	9.46	5.76	+/-S&P 500
+/-Russ MG	11.76	2.19	39.32	-6.56	-30.21	16.23	4.10	9.01	-7.95	26.87	2.27	10.89	+/-Russ MG
Income Return %	0.00	0.00	0.00	0.00	0.00	0.00	0.00	0.00	0.00	0.00	0.00	0.00	Income Return %
Capital Return %	45.68	19.67	61.86	11.30	21.06	4.48	-16.05	-18.40	34.76	42.35	14.37	21.55	Capital Return %
Total Rtn % Rank Cat (B)	14	30	1	66	83	37	46	17	55	1	18	2	Total Rtn % Rank Cat (B)
Income $	0.00	0.00	0.00	0.00	0.00	0.00	0.00	0.00	0.00	0.00	0.00	0.00	Income $
Capital Gains $	0.00	0.00	0.00	0.00	0.00	0.00	0.00	0.00	1.36	0.43	0.78	0.06	Capital Gains $
Expense Ratio % (H)	—	—	—	—	—	—	—	—	—	1.45	1.46	—	Expense Ratio % (H)
Income Ratio %	—	—	—	—	—	—	—	—	—	-1.79	-0.83	—	Income Ratio %
Turnover Rate % (H)	—	—	—	—	—	—	—	—	—	37	58	—	Turnover Rate % (H)
Net Assets $mil	—	—	—	—	—	—	—	—	164	633	2,302		Net Assets $mil

Rating and Risk

Time Period	Load-Adj Return %	Morningstar Rtn vs Cat	Morningstar Risk vs Cat	Morningstar Risk-Adj Rating
1 Yr	21.55			
3 Yr	25.54	High	+Avg	★★★★★
5 Yr	16.82	High	High	★★★★★
10 Yr	15.33	High	High	★★★
Incept	18.30			

Other Measures	Standard Index S&P 500	Best Fit Index DJ Wilshire 4500
Alpha	10.4	9.0 (F)
Beta	1.47	1.02 (E)
R-Squared	57	73

Standard Deviation	(D) 13.28
Mean	25.54
Sharpe Ratio	(G) 1.54

Portfolio Analysis 09-30-06

Share change since 03-06 Total Stocks:47	Sector	PE	Tot Ret%	% Assets
⊕ Wynn Resorts, Ltd.	Consumer	—	82.51	5.72
⊕ Las Vegas Sands, Inc.	Consumer	72.8	126.70	5.51
⊕ Boyd Gaming Corporation	Consumer	31.9	-3.73	4.74
⊕ Iron Mountain, Inc.	Business	45.5	-2.09	4.88
⊕ Jefferies Group, Inc.	Financial	19.6	21.21	4.39
⊖ Charles Schwab Corporati	Financial	26.1	32.87	4.24
⊕ Manor Care, Inc.	Health	24.6	19.65	4.21
⊕ AllianceBernstein Holdin	—	20.4	50.15	3.97
⊕ ChoicePoint, Inc.	Business	26.3	-11.53	3.39
✿ Fastenal Company	Business	28.0	-7.37	2.74
⊕ Chicago Mercantile Excha	Financial	46.9	39.48	2.72
⊕ International Securities	Financial	—	70.81	2.50
⊕ Nuveen Investments, Inc.	Financial	23.7	24.13	2.49
⊕ Toll Brothers, Inc.	Consumer	6.5	-6.96	2.36
Four Seasons Hotel, Inc.	Consumer	—	65.03	2.33
Dick's Sporting Goods, I	Consumer	26.9	47.38	2.27
✿ Brookdale Senior Living,	Health	—	—	2.20
⊕ Penn National Gaming	Goods	22.1	26.31	2.16
Arch Capital Group, Ltd	Financial	18.3	23.49	2.11
⊕ Whole Foods Market, Inc.	Consumer	33.3	37.19	2.04

Current Investment Style

Value Blend Growth

Market Cap	%
Giant	0.0
Large	21.1
Mid	64.7
Small	14.2
Micro	0.0

Avg $mil: 4,960

Value Measures		Rel Category
Price/Earnings	22.95	1.12
Price/Book	3.58	1.12
Price/Sales	2.23	1.27
Price/Cash Flow	13.72	1.20
Dividend Yield %	0.91	1.44

Growth Measures	%	Rel Category
Long-Term Erngs	16.14	0.99
Book Value	11.02	0.87
Sales	15.30	1.53
Cash Flow	19.25	1.04
Historical Erngs	27.15	1.05

Profitability	%	Rel Category
Return on Equity	18.08	1.01
Return on Assets	9.88	1.05
Net Margin	13.72	1.18

Sector Weightings

	% of Stocks	Rel S&P 500	3 Year High	Low
⟳ Info	0.00	0.00		
Software	0.00	0.00	0	0
Hardware	0.00	0.00	0	0
Media	0.00	0.00	4	0
Telecom	0.00	0.00	0	0
⟳ Service	90.38	1.96		
Health	8.58	0.71	9	5
Consumer	35.05	4.58	55	24
Business	17.82	4.21	24	17
Financial	28.93	1.30	36	17
⟳ Mfg	9.62	0.28		
Goods	5.73	0.67	6	1
Ind Mtrls	0.00	0.00	1	0
Energy	2.61	0.27	8	0
Utilities	1.28	0.37	2	0

Composition

	%
● Cash	0.0
● Stocks	99.3
● Bonds	0.0
● Other	0.7
Foreign	3.5
(% of Stock)	

Morningstar's Take by Kerry O'Boyle 12-07-06

Gambling anyone?

Baron Partners is the fund where veteran small- and mid-cap growth manager Ron Baron lets it all hang out. This fund, a former partnership that was converted into a mutual fund in 2003, can short stocks and use leverage (borrow money) to boost its equity exposure. It's the most compact offering that Baron runs at 47 holdings, and nearly 50% of the fund's assets are in its top 10 stocks. He's also willing to load up more here on the industries he thinks offer the greatest opportunity than he is at other, more-diversified offerings that he runs.

As evidence, more than 20% of assets, including the portfolio's top three holdings—Wynn Resorts, Las Vegas Sands, and Boyd Gaming—are devoted to casino operators. Baron, a longtime fan of these so-called "gaming" stocks, thinks that the price/earnings multiples for these fast-growing firms remain low because of the "sin" stigma attached to gambling. But Baron cites the continuing expansion of the industry across the U.S.

and overseas, with the building boom in Macau being the latest example of gaming's popularity. Thanks in large part to that bet, the fund's results thus far in 2006 have been spectacular. Its 23.5% gain for the year to date through December 4 bests its typical mid-growth rival by nearly 13 percentage points.

Investors should be aware, however, that this fund's style involves considerable risk. Although the fund currently has no short positions and is only minimally levered (104% invested), its concentrated positions can just as quickly turn south. The greater risk also causes Baron to trade a bit more here—a departure from his normally low-turnover style—in an attempt to keep volatility in check.

While Baron has proven himself to be a savvy stock-picker in his nearly 20 years as a mutual fund manager, this fund's aggressive profile is not for the faint of heart. Only the most risk-tolerant investors need apply.

Address:	767 Fifth Ave New York NY 10153 800-442-3814	Minimum Purchase:	$2000	Add: $0	IRA: $0
		Min Auto Inv Plan:	$500	Add: $50	
		(H) Sales Fees:	No-load, 0.25%S		
Web Address:	www.baronfunds.com	Management Fee:	1.00%		
Inception:	01-31-92	(H) Actual Fees:	Mgt 1.00%	Dist 0.25%	
Advisor:	Bamco Inc.	Expense Projections:	3Yr:$511	5Yr:$881	10Yr:$1922
Subadvisor:	None	Income Distrib:	Annually		
NTF Plans:	Fidelity Retail-NTF, Schwab OneSource				

Tenure

Tenure is the time spent (in years) by the portfolio manager on managing, directing, and implementing the strategies and investments of the managed fund. (Some mutual funds may not have a "portfolio manager" but indicate that the mutual fund is "managed by a team." If this happens with one or more of your mutual funds, call the fund directly and obtain the lead manager's name and tenure on the fund.)

Is tenure important? You bet! Tenure is important because it is the primary indicator for selecting the number of years or relevant time period to use to evaluate a mutual fund. The life of a mutual fund may exceed the tenure of the current portfolio manager. However, for evaluation purposes, the performance of a mutual fund is typically only important for the time that the current manager has been guiding the fund.

Refer to "C" in the Morningstar report. Ron Baron has managed the fund since its inception in 1992. If the manager's tenure is short (less than five years), you should attempt to ascertain where he or she was before and what fund or funds he or she managed and the level of performance achieved by those fund or funds. Do this by calling the current mutual fund.

Once the relevant time period is established—in this instance ten years—the next factor to examine is risk. How do you react when the market and your fund goes down? Are you equipped to handle the downside or negative returns that invariably creep into a fund's performance? The next two measures—standard deviation and beta—help you see how severely a mutual fund moved (positively and negatively) during a specific time period.

Standard Deviation and Beta

These two statistics are generally accepted as the two most often-used indices to measure risk. Risk in its simplest form is defined as the possibility of loss.

Standard deviation measures the difference between the actual returns of a fund (over time) and the average return for that fund over the same time period. It shows how far the actual returns deviate from the average return. The importance of standard deviation is that it accepts as a given the many factors that influence a fund's return. The larger the standard deviation, the further away from the average a typical return lies. The further away an actual return lies from the average return, the greater the risk associated with that mutual fund. This is evidenced by a high standard deviation number.

Refer to "D" in the Morningstar report. Baron Partners Fund has a standard deviation of 13.28 percent. (This calculation is based on data over the past thirty-six months.) This means that 68 percent of the returns of the fund fell between plus or minus 13.28 percent of its average return. Using the three-year average return of 25.5 percent, this range of returns is between +38.78 percent to +12.22 percent. This range is arrived at in the following manner:

Upper Range:

Take the average return of 25.5 percent and add the standard deviation of +13.28 percent. This yields an upper range of +38.78 percent. (Remember that standard deviation is both a positive and negative number.)

Lower Range:

Take the average return of 25.5 percent and subtract the standard deviation of-13.28 percent. This yields a lower range of +12.22 percent.

If you were looking for greater statistical accuracy, say 95 percent (or two standard deviations), the standard deviation would be plus or minus 26.56 percent. The upper and lower ranges would be +52.06 percent to-1.06 percent.

Another way to explain standard deviation is by comparing the grade-point average of two students, Alicia and Beth. Let's say Alicia's average was higher than Beth's. The conclusion that could be easily reached is that Alicia was a better overall student than Beth. But by investigating the details, we learn that Alicia's average was made up of more As and Cs but fewer Bs than Beth's. From the details, we can conclude that while Alicia's average was higher, her individual grades were more spread out than Beth's. So while Alicia's grade-point average was higher, she experienced greater risk in attaining that average (receiving more of the lower grade of C and thus requiring more A's.) Would you be comfortable taking on the added risk to possibly achieve a higher return?

Beta, on the other hand, measures the degree of variation or volatility of a fund's return in relation to a benchmark or market index given the numerous influences in the marketplace. (This benchmark index can be, for example, the S&P 500 or the Wilshire 4500.) The benchmark index always has a value of 1.00. This measure (beta) is important because it isolates the amount of risk in a fund that is caused by the benchmark index. In using this factor, utilize the "best fit" beta as the benchmark beta because it better reflects the underlying characteristics of the portfolio.

What does this mean? Beta is another measure of volatility and shows the degree of risk a fund possesses. Unlike standard deviation that shows the volatility inherent in a fund, beta compares the riskiness of a fund to that fund's benchmark index. However, a low beta doesn't necessarily mean that a fund has a low degree of volatility.[1] It means that the fund's market-related risk is low.[2] So, how do you know how much risk is market-related? This is supported by the r-squared (r^2) statistic. What is r^2 (called the coefficient of determination)? R^2 shows how much of a fund's return can be explained by the fund's "best fit" benchmark index.[3] The higher the r^2 of the fund, the higher the certainty that the fund's volatility is attributable to this benchmark index. The higher the r^2 the more relevant the

---

1. *Morningstar Principia Mutual Funds.* CD-ROM. March 2006.
2. Ibid.
3. Ibid.

beta is to the fund's return. (Other factors that can cause volatility that are outside beta include industry risk and company risk.)

Refer to "E" in the Morningstar report. Baron Partners Fund has a beta of 1.02 when measured against its benchmark index of the Wilshire 4500 and an r^2 of .73. (This calculation is based on data over the past thirty-six months.) What does this mean? It means that nearly three-quarters of the fund's beta or volatility is explained by the benchmark index. If, let's say, the Wilshire 4500 index gained 10 percent, the fund's return should theoretically rise 10.2 percent (which is 102 percent of the total increase). Conversely, if this index showed a 10 percent decline, the fund should theoretically drop 10.2 percent (or again by 102 percent of the decrease). Here, too, the higher the number, the greater the fund's volatility.

These two concepts—standard deviation and beta—are central to the mutual fund selection process. Once you've become comfortable with these two measures of risk and come to understand and accept the extent of variation or volatility you're able to cope with, your attention can then be turned to a fund's alpha statistic and Sharpe ratio.

Alpha

Alpha shows the ability of a fund to generate returns that are higher or lower than the fund's expected return given the fund's level of risk. The risk measure that underscores the determination of alpha is the fund's beta. The alpha is expressed as a percentage. The higher the positive number the better, the higher the negative number the worse. This is explained below.

The importance of alpha is that it represents a level of return generated by a mutual fund that is above or below the level the fund's beta would have predicted. To put it another way, alpha is a measure that shows how well the portfolio manager has done the job of managing the fund and adding incremental value beyond the fund's return expectations.

Refer to "F" in the Morningstar report. Baron Partners Fund's alpha was 9.0 percent when computed using the Wilshire 4500 index. (This calculation is based on data over the past thirty-six months.) This means that the fund outperformed or achieved a result in excess of the market's expectation. If the fund achieved the market's expectation, its alpha would have been equal to zero. If it underperformed the market's expectation, the number would have been negative.

Alpha can be found in many facets of daily life and certainly outside of the investment arena. For example, let's say you decide to take a two-week vacation. You put together a detailed itinerary that, when priced out, costs $10,000. This includes airfare, hotels, meals, entertainment, and other expenses. However, before making the arrangements, you visit a travel agent and ask the agent to price it out. The travel agent comes back with a price tag of $9,000. The alpha in this instance would be $1,000—the extra value the travel agent could bring to your vacation plans.

Sharpe Ratio

The **Sharpe ratio** measures the extent to which a mutual fund earns a return in excess of the return it was expected to achieve given the riskiness of the investment. In this instance, risk is measured by standard deviation (not beta). So for every 1 percent of standard deviation or risk taken, a certain level of excess return or shortfall, as expressed by the Sharpe ratio, is earned.

Refer to "G" in the Morningstar report. In the case of Baron Partners Fund, the Sharpe ratio is calculated to be 1.54. (This calculation is based on data over the past thirty-six months.) What this means to you if you were an investor in this mutual fund is that for every 1 percent of risk you agreed to accept, your reward or excess return was 1.54 percent.

To summarize the essence of the Alpha and Sharpe ratio statistics:

- Alpha gauges a mutual fund's performance relative to a benchmark index, such as the Wilshire 4500, and uses beta to measure that performance.

- The Sharpe ratio measures the performance of a mutual fund relative to its own risk characteristics and uses standard deviation to measure that performance.

Fund Fees, Expenses, and Other

The last measure is the **fund's fees and expenses** paid by the investor. This term is a catchall that includes several components. For the sake of argument, let's say you have narrowed your selection to three comparable mutual funds within a given category and style. Which would you choose? The measure that can be used to break this impasse could be the fees and expenses you would incur to have your money managed by this mutual fund.

Refer to "H" in the Morningstar report. ("H" appears in four spots.) Fees and expenses include:

Expense Ratio   This encompasses the management fee paid to the portfolio manager to manage the fund's investments as well as other charges, including miscellaneous administration and the 12b-1 fee. It is expressed as a percentage to the fund's price or net asset value (NAV) per share. Baron Partners Fund's annual expense ratio is not shown in the report for 2006. However, further investigation revealed it was 1.45 percent of its average NAV. Usually this fee is deducted daily. If, for example, your account value was $10,000, one day's fee would be 40 cents ($10,000 * 1.45 percent/365 days).

12b—1 Fee	This is a charge the fund makes for distribution and other related service activities. These can include marketing and selling costs and printing and mailing costs. Baron Partners Fund shows this fee to be .25 percent or one-quarter of 1 percent. This expense is included in the expense ratio of 1.45 percent.
Turnover Ratio	This shows the rapidity with which the portfolio manager buys and sells existing portfolio holdings and purchases new holdings for the fund. This report does not show the Baron Partners Fund's turnover ratio for 2006. Further analysis determined it was 38 percent. That is, nearly two-fifths of the entire portfolio is changed yearly. While there are no explicit costs that show the dollar impact of this activity, the higher the turnover ratio, the higher the trading costs and the greater the impact on the overall performance or return the fund achieves. (If you have a regular or individual account that's not an IRA or other form of tax-deferred account, trading or selling the holdings could cause you to owe taxes on the account.)
Front-End Load	An investor is charged this fee for using a commission-based broker or investment professional to purchase shares of a load fund. These are the A shares. Baron Partners Fund is a no-load fund and does not have share classes. (There is no up-front sales charge as you would have for A shares or a deferred sales charge that you would have with B and C shares.)
Deferred Load	This is a fee the investor pays *only* if B or C shares are sold or redeemed prematurely. There is no deferred load for A shares. B shares have a declining deferred load. Typically, the maximum period B shares must be held is six to seven years. The deferred load is a declining percentage that generally begins at 6 percent and every year (or on occasion every two years) declines one percentage point (or on occasion two percentage points), until after the sixth year there is no longer any restriction on selling the shares. Generally, after eight years the B shares convert to A shares. But let's say that after three years you decide to redeem your entire account valued at $10,000, a 3 percent charge, or $300, would be assessed against the sale proceeds. The net you would receive is $9,700. Furthermore, the expense ratio is higher than that of an A share, as well as a no-load fund. Typically, this difference is .75 percent.

C shares have a one-year waiting period before they can be sold without incurring an early redemption penalty. Typically, this penalty is 1 percent. In reality, though, the typical holding period for any mutual fund should be more than one year. So it would seem this potential cost is moot. (This 1 percent also is *not* reflected in the total return [percent] numbers.) As with B shares, the expense ratio of C shares is generally .75 percent higher than that of A shares as well as a no-load fund, and in many instances is equivalent to the B share expense ratio.

The foregoing statistical factors should be used for mutual funds that are in nontaxable accounts, such as IRAs, as well as taxable or individual accounts. There are, however, two additional statistics that should be considered when the mutual fund is in an individual account. In such an account, tax efficiency becomes important. As Warren Buffet has said, "It's not what you earn, it's what you keep." These statistics, which appear in the tax analysis section of the Morningstar report, are tax-cost ratio and potential capital gain exposure.

Tax Cost Ratio	Refer to "I" in the Morningstar report. This statistic shows the extent to which taxable distributions reduce the mutual fund's return. (This calculation assumes the investor pays the maximum federal tax rate on capital gains and ordinary income.) For the Baron Partners Fund, the three-year annualized tax-cost was .49 of 1 percent, compounded yearly. For the five-year and ten-year periods, the tax cost's annual compound rate was just over .6 percent and .3 percent, respectively.
Potential Capital Gain	Refer to "J" in the Morningstar report. This statistic is an estimate of the percent of the mutual fund's assets that come from the increase in value of the stocks in the portfolio. It also indicates the level of potential taxable capital gain distribution. For the Baron Partners Fund, the potential capital gain exposure to fund holders is 27 percent or $622 million of the total assets of $2,302 million (see reference "K" in the Morningstar report).

WHICH MUTUAL FUND TO CHOOSE?

Like any other person about to invest, you likely have many questions about how to choose the right mutual funds. Do you just look at "Percentile Rank in Category/Mean" and then choose? What about risk? Do you use standard deviation? Isn't beta a good factor to use? Should you consider the alpha statistic in choosing? Do you ignore the Sharpe ratio? What about fund fees and expenses? You've compiled all the statistics. How do you feel about using other factors in addition to percentile rank in category/mean to select your mutual funds? To put it another way, do you feel comfortable going beyond the ranking of a fund and its rate of return achieved?

It's reasonable to say that the higher your risk profile score, the less emphasis you may place on the risk measures and the more emphasis you would place on the percentile rank/mean statistic. However, risk should not be completely dismissed regardless of how high your risk profile score is. Always lurking in the shadows is the possibility that the market could experience a downturn. Just think back to 2000–02, the "tech bubble."

Finalizing your selection of mutual funds has many similarities to teaching your child to swim. Your child has been in the water with you, doing virtually everything short of swimming alone. She's floated in the water, but you've held her head. She has kicked in the water using a floatation board, but you were there. She has submerged her head in the water and held her breath, but you were right beside her. She has kept her eyes open underwater, but you were next to her. Now she's at the edge of the pool. You have moved away. You can sense her trepidation. Is she going to leap in? The comparable sink-or-swim question for you as an investor is: do you select your mutual funds on your own or do you seek a financial advisor? One difference between the two situations is that your daughter has an immediate support system, whatever her decision. With your mutual fund selection, it could be years later before you find out if you made a good decision. At that time will there be a support mechanism? (A difference of just one or two percentage points in return over thirty years could easily mean hundreds of thousands of dollars in account value.)

Most probably you're going to make your own decision based on your experiences and using the data with which you are comfortable. Or maybe you are going to seek a financial advisor. In either case, a decision will be made. Just be sure your decisions are not driven by something overheard at the water cooler or by blindly selecting something.

SUMMARY

The initial phase in selecting mutual funds for your portfolio is determining the goal for the investment and your risk tolerance. These two factors should be kept in mind while selecting and evaluating the mutual funds. These factors become even more important in understanding asset allocation and portfolio construction. When selecting mutual funds for review, recording the key factors of those mutual funds is crucial. Mutual funds should be analyzed by category and style. For example, all large cap value funds should be on the same technical analysis worksheet.

For emphasis, the key factors are summarized below:

1. Percentile rank in category/mean (percent return)

2. Tenure of the portfolio manager

3. Risk:

    *   Standard deviation

    *   Beta

4. Alpha

5. Sharpe ratio

6. Fund fees, expenses, and other

    For Taxable Accounts:

7. Tax Cost Ratio

8. Potential Capital Gain Exposure

Once you've recorded the information on the statistical analysis worksheets, the evaluation of each mutual fund's statistics against each other is done in a manner consistent with the definition and explanations of each measure. Now you must make certain decisions. It's up to you to balance the qualitative measures and the statistical factors and select those mutual funds that are most consistent with your profile. A note: It's possible one or more of your initial mutual fund selections may be changed prior to finalizing your portfolio. However, don't assume that once your mutual fund portfolio is established, you will have to monitor your portfolio on a daily basis. You won't! Monthly or quarterly monitoring may be more appropriate. You must find your level of comfort and confidence in your mutual fund selections and the actions of the market.

Chapter 3:

Asset Allocation

○ ○

Diversification is your buddy.

—Merton Miller
Economist and Nobel laureate

Congratulations! You deserve to be applauded. The chapter you just completed on selecting mutual funds was difficult but crucial to the overall process and key to the following chapter, "Portfolio Construction." You now have the tools that facilitate your effort to select the mutual funds for your investment portfolio.

The purpose of this chapter on asset allocation is to give you a basic understanding of the importance of allocating your investment dollars among different categories and styles of mutual funds. This chapter will be followed by chapters on constructing your mutual fund portfolio and monitoring and rebalancing or reallocating your portfolio.

Simply put, asset allocation is the balancing of an investment portfolio among stock mutual funds, bond mutual funds, and cash. (Be aware that asset allocation does not ensure a profit and does not protect against losses in a declining market). To begin to understand asset allocation, two questions need to be answered at the outset:

1. Why is it important to balance or allocate your investment portfolio?

2. What has academic research offered that demonstrates the degree, if any, mutual fund portfolio returns are affected by asset allocation?

But first, let's begin with an example of asset allocation in action.

A COMPARATIVE EXAMPLE OF THE ASSET ALLOCATION PROCESS IN ACTION

Asset allocation, in many ways, is like planning a wedding. The real value is in the details. In asset allocation, you delineate your investments into two styles—value and growth. (While blend funds represent a third style, it is excluded from this discussion. Blend funds are a combination of value and growth.) You then refine each style by segmenting them into categories that include domestic equity funds, international equity funds, and bonds. The categories and styles can be further defined by the size of the fund's holdings—large cap, mid-cap, and small cap. From this point, you determine the amount of your total investment that should go into each component to attain that optimal portfolio or result. In planning a wedding, there are two significant areas of concern—the ceremony and the reception. From here, you break down each area into those components that could affect the outcome of the wedding. You then attempt to determine the impact each component could have on the wedding and apportion to each component the necessary time, attention, and money to achieve an optimal result—a flawless wedding.

IMPORTANCE OF ASSET ALLOCATION

Asset allocation functions as a risk control mechanism. It seeks to reduce the effects of market volatility by attempting to balance risk among a portfolio's investments. (Generally, the risk of loss associated with stocks or stock mutual funds is greater than that of bonds or bond mutual funds. And the risk of loss associated with bonds or bond mutual funds is greater than that of cash.) Asset allocation is one of the primary means for attempting to manage risk at a level that is comfortable for you. Asset allocation attempts to address three significant areas of investor concern:

1. Your investment goals and objectives

2. Your tolerance for risk

3. Your time requirements for the funds

Once you've answered the above investor concerns, you can proceed to allocate your assets based on:

1. The best combination of stock mutual funds and bond mutual funds

2. The most appropriate blend between domestic mutual funds and international mutual funds

3. The most suitable mix of stock mutual funds among large cap, mid-cap, and small cap, as well as value and growth funds

The next chapter, "Portfolio Construction," provides answers that address these specific points to best meet your needs.

QUANTITATIVE IMPACT OF ASSET ALLOCATION

The conclusion reached in a 1986 watershed study[1] and confirmed in a 1991 follow-up study[2] was that asset allocation was responsible for a significant portion of the variation in quarterly portfolio returns. Since the 1991 study, there have been several other papers[3] that have validated the conclusions reached in 1986 and 1991. However, the degree or magnitude of the impact remains in question and will probably be debated for years. (You don't have to go any further than the "tech bubble" of 2000–02 to see the effect of asset allocation or a lack of asset allocation. If you were fully invested

---

1. Brinson, Gary P., Randolph Hood, Gilbert L. Beebower. "Determinants of Portfolio Performance." *Financial Analysts Journal,* July/August 1986.

    This seminal study on asset allocation involved the analysis of ninety-one large pension funds from 1974–83. The study concluded that on average 93.6 percent of the quarterly variation in plan results was attributed to asset allocation. Furthermore, the study concluded that less than 5 percent in the quarterly variation of plan results was caused by security selection.

2. Brinson, Gary P., Brian D. Singer, Gilbert L. Beebower. "Determinants of Portfolio Performance II: An Update." *Financial Analysts Journal,* May/June 1991.

    In this study, the impact of passive and active asset allocation and security selection was analyzed. This analysis studied eighty-two large pension plans that covered the period 1977–87. It concluded that passive asset allocation explained 91.5 percent of the variation in quarter-to-quarter portfolio returns.

and concentrated in technology stocks or technology mutual funds during this time, you probably lost a significant portion of your portfolio's value. Most probably, that loss was greater than if your assets were allocated among several categories and styles of investment.)

OTHER REASONS FOR ASSET ALLOCATION

An underlying rationale for asset allocation is that the investment category or style that ends up at year-end to be the market leader is not easily predictable. Through the use of asset allocation, however, you're able to participate in the overall success of the market and at the same time possibly reduce your risk of loss. This is because all types of investments don't move in the same direction or to the same extent or have the same risk characteristics.

This is demonstrated in the Callan Periodic Table of Investment Returns. This table shows the returns achieved by each category, large, mid-, and small capitalization companies, and style, value, and growth of investment. For the current twenty-year period, 1987–2006, in only one instance did one category and style lead the pack for more than two consecutive years. From 1995 through 98, large company stocks achieved returns of 38.1 percent, 24 percent, 36.5 percent, and 42.2 percent,

---

3.   Jahnke, William. "The Asset Allocation Hoax." *Journal of Financial Planning,* February 1997.

This analysis revisited the Brinson, Hood, and Beebower study of 1986 and found it to be flawed. According to the author, the 1986 study focused on portfolio volatility and not on portfolio returns. Because of this, the average percentage cited—93.6 percent—pertained to the variation in quarterly results and not the variation in the rate of returns. The conclusion reached by the author was that asset allocation explained only 14.6 percent of the total return (not the 93.6 percent noted in the 1986 study).

Singer, Brian. "Hoax and Strawmen." *Journal of Financial Planning,* October 1997.

Evensky, Harold. "The Hoax Is a Hoax." *Financial Planning,* November 1997.

Wilson, Philip. "Mad As Hell." *Dow Jones Investment Advisor,* February 1998.

Beebower, Gilbert, Michael Hogan, Robert Ludwig. "Asset Allocation: Is it a Hoax?" *SEI,* spring 1998.

Statman, Meir. "The Numbers Racket Rages On." *Financial Planning,* April 1998.

Ibbotson, Roger G., and Paul D. Kaplan. "Does Asset Allocation Policy Explain 40, 90, or 100 Percent of Performance?" Available at www.ibbotson.com/research, December 1998, revised April 1999.

"Asset Allocation: Revisiting the Debate." Morningstar, February 27, 1997.

respectively. Predicting the category and style of investment that will lead the pack by year's end is much like trying to pick the winning lottery number. A few may be fortunate, but many will be utterly disappointed.

ADVANTAGES AND DISADVANTAGES OF ASSET ALLOCATION

There are essentially two fundamental advantages that asset allocation offers:[4]

1. A means to attempt to optimize the return on your investment portfolio. You seek to maximize your portfolio return according to the level of risk you believe you can tolerate.

2. A way to create and control risk by avoiding the proverbial "putting all your eggs into one basket."

The one major disadvantage of asset allocation is the possibility of missing opportunities.[5] For example, during the period 1995 to 1998, if your investment portfolio was concentrated in large cap holdings, your average yearly return would have exceeded 35 percent. In all likelihood, this level of return exceeded that of any portfolio allocated among large cap, mid-cap, small cap, and international holdings. However, to have anticipated such a recurrence, particularly for four consecutive years, was highly remote, if not impossible.

RISK PROFILE QUESTIONNAIRE

Three factors are the primary drivers in the determination of asset allocation. These factors are your investment goals and objectives, your risk tolerance, and your expectation of the time needed to achieve the intended result.

Before you consider the risk and time factors, it is important that you clearly define your goals and objectives for the portfolio. For example, your goals could include but certainly are not limited to:

1. Retirement

2. Supplemental income

3. Education of children or grandchildren

4. Special purchase, such as a vacation home or an extended vacation

---

4.   Darst, David M. *The Art of Asset Allocation.* (New York: The McGraw-Hill Companies, 2003), 11.
5.   Ibid.

In trying to come to terms with your tolerance for risk, I recommend you use a questionnaire with questions that delve into basic feelings about taking risks. An example of such a questionnaire appears at the end of this chapter. When answering the questions, your responses should be consistent with and be reflective of your intended goals for the portfolio. They should incorporate your feelings and thoughts when it comes to the possible loss of a portion of your portfolio's value. And, of course, your replies should be made with due consideration given to the amount of time the portfolio will have to grow. (Typically, the longer the time horizon to achieve your goals, the more tolerant of risk you may be.)

The Risk Profile Questionnaire[6] comprises eight questions. The first seven questions are in standard format. That is, each question presents an issue and offers possible replies. You select the response that is most suitable and comfortable for you. The last question, however, is in tabular form. It shows four hypothetical portfolios and the returns they achieve over a five-year period. Even though a five-year period is shown, the four portfolio options should be examined together for each year. To do this, cover up the years that remain to be examined. Then gauge your reaction to each hypothetical portfolio's performance and select the portfolio best suited for you before you proceed to the next year. This should be done for each of the five years. There are no correct answers. The purpose of this questionnaire is to show tendencies and to find a consistent pattern to your responses.

After a detailed examination of your answers (combined with your selected mutual funds), the next step is to create a diversified portfolio that meets your needs and goals. (That's easier said than done. But we'll do it!) Try to find the kind of portfolio that gives you the maximum expected return for the least amount of risk assumed (as measured by standard deviation)—the optimal return. The stock mutual fund portion of your portfolio generally includes more categories and styles of investment than the bond mutual fund portion. Because of this complexity, I find it easier in the development of an investment portfolio to begin with the fixed component. Based on the risk profile score achieved from the questionnaire, the following table presents a guideline on the relative size of the fixed component or bond mutual fund portion that should be considered for your investment portfolio.

Risk Profile Score	Suggested Percent of Bonds
Maximum Growth: 22–24	3%–0%
Growth: 18–21	15%–6%
Conservative Growth: 14–17	44%–21%
Income: 10–13	58%
Conservative Income: 7–9	75%

---

6. Portions were adapted from the one used at H. D. Vest Financial Services in Irving, Texas.

SUMMARY

In many ways, asset allocation is like various things we do in everyday life. The example of planning a wedding has many similarities to asset allocation because it involves appropriately apportioning a certain amount of money to many activities. The end result, of course, is to have a special wedding.

Whether it's planning a wedding, devising a family expense budget, or creating an investment portfolio, asset allocation is important because it can be used to construct an optimal result: where the intended result is the highest achievable given a certain level of risk. In asset allocation, you're spreading your investment over a variety of opportunities as opposed to concentrating it in only one or two opportunities. So even though maximizing your return may not be possible, you should be able to reduce your downside risk exposure.

An effective way of determining the level of risk you can tolerate is by using the Risk Profile Questionnaire. This survey seeks replies to questions that, when analyzed, can be translated into your risk profile score. This risk profile score functions as a starting point in creating your asset allocation.

However, when it comes to quantifying the benefit asset allocation offers, it becomes a little tenuous, as the various referenced studies indicated. But while the exact benefit remains elusive, these academic studies undoubtedly show that there is a quantifiable benefit.

RISK PROFILE QUESTIONNAIRE

_____   _____
                Name   Date

There are no right or wrong answers. Simply check the answer that is most representative.
The following answers are not to be construed as investment instructions in the event that the scenarios depicted actually occur.

1. How long do you think you will retain this investment portfolio?

   [ ] 1   *3 to 5 years*
   [ ] 2   *5 to 10 years*
   [ ] 3   *over 10 years*

2. Although past performance is no guarantee of future results, stocks or stock mutual funds have historically provided better protection against inflation than bonds or bond mutual funds. And through diversification, a portfolio of stocks or stock mutual funds also provides the potential for less volatility in returns. But historically, stock or stock mutual funds have been more volatile than bond or bond mutual funds. How do you feel about stocks or stock mutual funds?

   [ ] 1   *I don't want them in my portfolio.*
   [ ] 2   *I would use them in my portfolio.*
   [ ] 3   *I think stock or stock mutual funds are very attractive and should occupy a dominant position in my portfolio.*

3. Is it important for you to receive money from your account on a monthly basis?

   [ ] 1   Yes, it is very important and it must be the same amount each month.
   [ ] 2   It is important, but growth of my portfolio is also an important factor.
   [ ] 3   It is not important, because growth of my portfolio is my primary goal.

4. Your feelings about investing can best be summed up as:

   [ ] 1   I would accept a moderate long-term rate of return rather than worry about my account losing money.
   [ ] 2   I can accept fluctuations in my account value if it means a higher potential return over the long run.
   [ ] 3   I want the maximum opportunity for long-term growth in my account and I am willing to accept significant year-to-year fluctuations in the value of my account.

5. Six months after you make a $100,000 investment it decreases in value by $15,000 in a down market period. How would you feel?

   [ ] 1   Very uncomfortable. I would consider selling my investment.
   [ ] 2   Uncomfortable, yet I would stay with the investment if my financial advisor recommended it.
   [ ] 3   I would want to buy more of the investment, since this is a good investment opportunity.

6. While small companies tend to have higher expected returns, they typically add more risk to your portfolio. How do you feel about having small companies in your portfolio?

   [ ] 1   I don't want to add more risk to my portfolio.
   [ ] 2   If my advisor recommends its, I would agree to it.
   [ ] 3   Should be used to appropriately allocate my portfolio. And, I am aware of the increased risk.

RISK PROFILE QUESTIONNAIRE

_____   _____
                Name   Date

7. A well diversified portfolio generally includes overseas investments. However, that could add more risk to your portfolio, particularly in the short-term. How do you feel about having overseas holdings in your portfolio?

☐ 1	I don't want to add more risk to my portfolio.
☐ 2	If my advisor recommends its, I would agree to it.
☐ 3	Should be used to appropriately allocate my portfolio. And, I am aware of the increased risk.

8. Below is a table showing five years of hypothetical returns for four hypothetical portfolios, A to D. A to D get progressively riskier. With which hypothetical portfolio do you feel most comfortable? (**Please note:** The rates of return shown below are purely hypothetical and do not represent the performance of any individual investment or portfolio of investments. They are for illustrative purposes only and should not be used to predict future product performance. Specific rates of return, especially for extended time periods, will vary over time. There is also a higher degree of risk associated with investments that offer the potential for higher rates of return.)

Instruction:

LOOK AT EACH SELECTION FOR THE 5-YEAR PERIOD. LOOK AT EACH YEAR CONSECUTIVELY. HOW DO YOU FEEL AFTER EACH YEAR? WITH WHICH TREND ARE YOU THE MOST COMFORTABLE AND TOLERANT, GIVEN THE FACT THAT YOU'RE NOT SUPPOSED TO KNOW WHAT THE FOLLOWING YEAR OR YEARS WILL BRING?

		Invest Now	Year 1	Year 2	Year 3	Year 4	Year 5	Average
A	0	$100,000	$103,000 (+3%)	$106,100 (+3%)	$109,300 (+3%)	$112,600 (+3%)	$115,900 (+3%)	3.0%
B	1	$100,000	$106,000 (+6%)	$106,000 (0%)	$96,500 (-9%)	$110,000 (+14%)	$117,700 (+7%)	3.6%
C	2	$100,000	$110,000 (+10%)	$103,400 (-6%)	$83,800 (-19%)	$108,900 (+30%)	$120,900 (+11%)	5.2%
D	3	$100,000	$111,000 (+11%)	$93,200 (-16%)	$74,600 (-20%)	$108,100 (+45%)	$122,200 (+15%)	7.0%

Standard Deviation is a statistical measure of risk and volatility. The higher the number the higher the risk and volatility associated with a portfolio. Portfolio A, B, C and D have the following Standard Deviations:

Portfolio	Standard Dev.	Explanation
A	0.000	There is no measurable risk and volatility.
B	7.645	2/3's of the yearly results (or between 3 and 4 years out of the total 5 years) fall within +11.245% and -4.045%.
C	16.600	2/3's of the yearly results (or between 3 and 4 years out of the total 5 years) fall within +21.800% and -11.400%.
D	23.567	2/3's of the yearly results (or between 3 and 4 years out of the total 5 years) fall within +30.567% and -16.567%.

Add the numbers from the answers that were checked in questions 1 - 8. Place that total on the line preceded by "Risk Profile Questionnaire Score." See below. Compare that number to those arranged and classified in the "Investor Profile." See below.

RISK PROFILE QUESTIONNAIRE SCORE _____

INVESTOR PROFILE

	Risk Profile Score		Risk Profile Score
Conservative Income	7 - 9	Growth	18 - 21
Income	10 - 13	Maximum Growth	22 - 24
Conservative Growth	14 - 17		

Chapter 4:

Portfolio Construction

Constructing a portfolio requires a process that will help you allocate your investment dollars among mutual funds you have selected. The result should be a portfolio that has an expected return consistent with your investment goals and objectives, your tolerance for risk, and your time requirements.

Portfolio construction starts with a pool of investment dollars. This pool should be initially allocated among stock mutual funds, bond mutual funds, and possibly cash. After this allocation is established, the process moves to greater specificity and detail. That is, for stock mutual funds, it means allocating investment dollars to your selected domestic funds which include large, mid-, and small capitalization categories and international funds. These fund categories are further divided between two styles: value-oriented funds and growth-oriented funds. (As mentioned earlier, blend funds, real estate investment trusts, and sector and country funds are not included in the discussion.)

The result of such allocation should be the highest expected return (percent return), given consideration to the statistical factors and your level of risk (standard deviation). This is called your optimal portfolio. However, for many of us, this optimal portfolio may have a level of risk that could still be too high. If you need a portfolio that has a lower degree of risk—a level of risk that provides greater comfort and less volatility—that's perfectly fine. (This may, however, result in a lower expected return.)

At the outset, it was mentioned that this book would *not* be a theoretical discussion, destined to sit on your library shelf. Rather, it is intended to be a useable guide that offers a process for constructing your investment portfolio. While there is a theoretical basis that forms the core of its content, theory is not used to explain any suggestions that are made here or material that was left out.

PORTFOLIO CONSTRUCTION ASSUMPTIONS

1. As a general rule, the greater the portion of your portfolio that is dedicated to bond funds or cash, the lower the level of risk and, consequently, the lower the potential return.

2. Even though a significant part of the total stock market's capitalization value resides with large companies (approximately 70 percent), it doesn't mean that 70 percent of your portfolio should be in large company mutual funds. Actually, the number of companies that make up the large company universe is minor (around 7 percent) when compared to the total number of companies that comprise the market.

3. Large cap and mid-cap holdings should consume relatively comparable investment dollars in your portfolio. From this it could be concluded that both categories have similar performance characteristics. They don't! This is illustrated on the next page as a continuation of point six.

4. Holdings in small cap and international funds should be nearly equal.

5. The level of fixed holdings that your portfolio should contain is noted in chapter 3 on asset allocation, immediately preceding the chapter's summary. As your risk profile score gets lower, your stock mutual fund holdings should decrease, and your bond mutual fund holdings should increase.

6. With regards to apportioning your investment between value and growth, the following is suggested:

•   For large and mid-cap holdings, a 3–7 percentage point differential that favors value is suggested. This differential should be relatively consistent from the maximum growth (24–22) risk profile through the conservative growth (17–14) risk profile. However, the value-growth difference should become narrower as you progress through the income (13–10) risk profile and the conservative income (9–7) risk profile. Over time, value-oriented large and mid-cap holdings have shown superior results to growth-oriented holdings. For the period 1994–2003, using Russell Investments statistical data for various stock market indices, the following results were computed. An initial investment of $10,000 in 1994 grew to the following levels by 2003 (excluding dividend or capital gain reinvestment):

	Value	Growth
Large Capitalization Holdings	$30,767	$23,814
Mid-Capitalization Holdings	$34,085	$24,597

This result, however, doesn't preclude the fact that growth funds should be sufficiently represented in your portfolio. All you have to do is remember the period 1995–98. During that time, returns from large cap growth led all categories and styles. And in 1999, small cap growth dominated investment returns.

• For small cap holdings, the line that delineates value from growth is blurry. It's conceivable that holdings that are considered value or growth today, could be different tomorrow. And while the historical performance of value exceeded growth, it is suggested that close to a one-to-one relationship is maintained in the portfolio whatever your risk profile score is.

• The international exposure was capped at 20 percent. However, as your risk profile score declines, your international exposure also should decline. A number of uncertainties exist when it comes to investing overseas. Foreign risk typically includes currency risk, political risk, accuracy of financial data risk, and risk associated with government actions. And while the degree of risk depends on where the investments are made, a cap of 20 percent is suggested.

7. Here is a starting point on details of the maximum growth portfolio.

The initial asset allocation shown on the next page offers great potential but with inherent risks. The historic return and standard deviation data that's shown in Schedule A, Revision to Initial Allocation Worksheet, (shown later) is from the Russell Investments Web site. The maximum growth portfolio (risk profile score 24) is fully invested in stock mutual funds. There are no bond mutual funds or cash holdings.

8. Here is a recap of portfolio construction assumptions.

The success of your portfolio can be directly related to the level of risk that is comfortable for you (as measured by standard deviation). This is a function of your asset allocation and selected mutual funds. To seek your desired outcome, you may have to go through several iterations of portfolio adjustments. But remember to keep your eye on the ball, namely the risk level and expected return, and be aware of the relative differences in weightings between value and growth holdings.

INITIAL ASSET ALLOCATION

Category and Style	Allocation
Large Cap Mutual Funds	
Value	18%
Growth	12%
Total Large Cap	**30%**
Mid-Cap Mutual Funds	
Value	18%
Growth	12%
Total Mid-Cap	**30%**
Small Cap Mutual Funds	
Value	10%
Growth	10%
Total Small Cap	**20%**
International	**20%**
Fixed	**0%**
Total	**100%**

QUANTIFYING YOUR INITIAL ALLOCATION

The upper limit of the maximum growth portfolio range has a risk profile score of 24. This establishes the baseline for your initial allocation. The result of this asset allocation using the Russell composite data shows a weighted historic return of 12.86 percent and a standard deviation of 18.924. For illustrative purposes, this data is used in lieu of the data that would be obtained by you from your mutual fund selections. Use the Schedule A, Revision to Initial Asset Allocation Worksheet, to quantify your initial allocation:

1. In column 1, list the names of your selected mutual funds by category and style.

2. In column 2, titled "Initial Asset Allocation (Profile Score 24)," do nothing.

3. In column 3, replace the existing historic return and historic standard deviation numbers with those from the Morningstar Mutual Fund reports for each of your selected mutual funds. Select each fund's time period to use based on the portfolio manager's tenure on the fund. For example, if the manager's tenure was greater than three years but not more than four years, use the three-year average return. If it was greater than five years but eight years or less, use the five-year average return. (Reference annotation B and C in the Morningstar Mutual Fund report for return and standard deviation information. This information for your selected mutual funds will be found in the same location.)

4. In column 4, calculate the weighted portions of the historic return and standard deviation for each of your selected mutual funds. This is done by multiplying the figures in column 2 with the historic return and historic standard deviation you just placed in column 3.

5. Sum both sets of numbers in column 4. The weighted results represent the historic weighted return and standard deviation for your maximum growth portfolio.

Excellent! Congratulations on making those calculations. What's your reaction to the portfolio's weighted return? What about the weighted standard deviation? Are they too high? Too low? Are you comfortable with them? Just to reiterate, this new standard deviation means that 68 percent of the returns fell between the return plus or minus the standard deviation. Are you comfortable with that range? Many people aren't. If not, adjustments are needed.

ILLUSTRATING THE ADJUSTMENT PROCESS

The rule that guides adjustments is that as you increase your bond mutual fund holdings, you decrease your stock mutual fund holdings. This typically leads to a lower standard deviation but also a lower historic return. Use Schedule B, Portfolio Construction Worksheet, to make adjustments.

From Schedule A, columns 1, 2 and 3, copy the names of your selected funds, the initial asset allocation and the historic returns and standard deviations to Schedule B, columns 1, 2 and 3. (Your selected mutual funds have been temporarily identified on the worksheets as "ABC," "DEF," etc. Replace those names with the names of your selected mutual funds. There are also numbers used for illustrative purposes in column 3; they were the original historic returns and standard deviations. Replace them with your revised numbers that now populate Schedule A, column 3.)

Schedule A
Revision to Initial Asset Allocation Worksheet

(1)	(2)	(3)		(4)	
	Initial Asset Allocation	**10-Year**		**Weighted Component**	
Category and Style/Fund Name	(Profile Score 24)	Historic Return	Historic Standard Deviation	Historic Return	Historic Standard Deviation
Large Cap					
Value_____	18%	12%	16.8	2.16%	3.024
Growth_____	12%	11%	20.9	1.32%	2.508
Total Large Cap	30%				
Mid-Cap					
Value_____	18%	14%	19.9	2.52%	3.582
Growth_____	12%	13%	23.5	1.56%	2.82
Total Mid-Cap	30%				
Small Cap					
Value_____	10%	14%	21.5	1.40%	2.15
Growth_____	10%	13%	24.0	1.30%	2.4
Total Small Cap	20%				
International_____	20%	13%	12.2	2.60%	2.44
Fixed_____	0%	7%	7.6	0.00%	0
Total	100%				
Weighted Results				12.86%	18.924

Schedule B
Portfolio Construction Worksheet

| | (1) | (2) | (3) | | (4) | (5) | |
| | | Initial Allocation (Risk Profile Score of 24) | Historic | | Revised Allocations | Revised Historic | |
Category/ Style	Selected Funds		Return	Standard Deviation		Return	Standard Deviation
Large Cap							
Value	ABC	18%	12.0%	16.8	13%	1.56%	2.184
Growth	DEF	12%	11.0%	20.9	7%	0.77%	1.463
Total Large Cap		30%			20%		
Mid-Cap							
Value	GHI	18%	14.0%	19.9	13%	1.82%	2.587
Growth	JKL	12%	13.0%	23.5	6%	0.78%	1.410
Total Mid-Cap		30%			19%		
Small Cap							
Value	MNO	10%	14.0%	21.5	5%	0.70%	1.075
Growth	PQR	10%	13.0%	24.0	4%	0.52%	0.960
Total Small Cap		20%			9%		
International	STU	20%	13.0%	12.2	8%	1.04%	0.976
Fixed	VWX	0%	7.0%	7.6	44%	3.08%	3.344
Total		100%			100%		
Weighted Results			12.86%	18.924		10.27%	13.999

Based on your understanding of standard deviation, have you decided on the standard deviation that gives you comfort? Is it 15? How about 11? Maybe 7? Once you've selected that standard deviation, record it on Schedule B, column 5, on the line for "Weighted Results." As a point of reference, I've included in Schedule B, column 4, a revised asset allocation that could represent a risk profile score of 14. This new asset allocation was completed by first increasing the bond component to reflect the data shown at the end of chapter 3 on asset allocation. In this instance, that was 44 percent. Similarly, the percentage allocations for all the categories and styles of your stock mutual fund selections were modified in column 4. (Remember, maintain appropriate differentials between value and growth holdings.) Follow the guidelines discussed under Portfolio Construction Assumptions. Please note, if your change in bond holdings is minor—for example, if you go from 0 percent to 3 percent—only reduce your small cap holdings.

Calculate the weighted results for column 5—the historic return and standard deviation. This is done by multiplying the values in column 4 with those in column 3. For instance, to compute the weighted result for the historic return, do the following: start with large cap value, and multiply the allocation of 13 percent by your historic return. Record the result in column 5 under "Return." Do the same for your other mutual fund selections. After completing this, add the individual results. This gives you the weighted historic return using the revised allocation. Repeat this process to calculate the historic standard deviation.

The process must be repeated if the results still do not meet your expectation for return and standard deviation. (Again, start by adjusting your bond component.) Continue this process until you've achieved the standard deviation you desire. Are you comfortable with the associated historic return? If you are, there's no need to do any more iterations. There you go! You've created your portfolio.

If you're happy with the weighted standard deviation but unhappy with the weighted return, then you should revisit your Risk Profile Questionnaire responses. Review your answers. Are any of your replies different now? If so, your risk profile score will change and result in a different allocation of stock and bond mutual funds. (Remember, it will also change your standard deviation.) If this is the case, change your allocations in column 4. Continue this process until you're satisfied with the standard deviation as well as the return.

SUMMARY

There's no denying it: portfolio construction is hard work. However, there is a starting point. This starting point reflects a risk profile score of 24, the maximum growth portfolio. Once the exercise of transferring data from your selected mutual funds to Schedule A, Revision to Initial Allocation Worksheet, and Schedule B, Portfolio Construction Worksheet, is completed, you are in a position to modify the "maximum growth portfolio" asset allocation to be more in line with your needs. Based on your determination of the degree of risk you're comfortable with (that's represented by standard deviation), you can begin the portfolio adjustment process. To assist you in this portfolio adjustment process, you should follow the portfolio construction assumptions. By reallocating the components of the portfolio and recalculating the historic return and standard deviation, you will eventually design a portfolio that's right for you. It will reflect an asset allocation that's consistent with your level for risk and a historic return that is to your liking.

Chapter 5:

Monitoring and Rebalancing or Reallocating

o o o o o o o o o o o o o o o o o o o o o o o o o o o o o o o o o o o o o o o o o

The stock market is not totally efficient.

—Scott M. Black
Delphi Management, Inc.

Believe it or not, you have just constructed your mutual fund portfolio. Outstanding! You should now be aware of the importance of allocating your investment assets as opposed to investing them into just one holding. At this point, you may ask, "Am I done?" Well, no! As the old song goes, "We've only just begun...."[1]

The world is not static. The world is not perfect. The economy is constantly changing. When it comes to your investments, that is also true. Things are changing at lightning speed. Information is flowing at nanospeed. To give asset allocation a chance, you must maintain vigilance over your investment portfolio. Your selections were made and your portfolio was constructed using historic

---

1.   Recorded by The Carpenters. Released August 21, 1970, A&M Records.

information. While history remains a good indicator of what might happen in the future, it's not a perfect one. It's important that you regularly monitor your portfolio and make the appropriate adjustments or rebalance it to maintain the asset allocation on which you spent so much time and effort constructing. If your personal situation significantly changes, you may need to reallocate your investment portfolio.

MONITORING

Webster's defines monitoring as "to check or sometimes to adjust." A more useable financial definition shows monitoring to be a process of periodically reviewing the performance of your portfolio and comparing its asset allocation to your predetermined asset allocation. Consistent with this definition, you should regularly assess the performance of your investment portfolio and the details related to its performance. You chose the mutual funds that comprise your portfolio based on selected statistical factors. Has the percentile rank in category of each of your mutual funds continued to maintain or better the standard used during the evaluation process? If it hasn't, you should attempt to determine the reasons for its lower performance. Are the same portfolio managers in place who were managing the mutual funds when you made your selections? Risk is always a concern. Have any of the selected mutual funds become unacceptably riskier? Have their standard deviations or betas increased? If the riskiness of any of the mutual funds changed, what has happened to their alpha and Sharpe ratios? And finally, have fees and expenses, including turnover, changed? These are key variables you should re-measure and compare against the standards originally used. Its an ongoing process.

REBALANCING

Actual performance of your mutual funds may cause your asset allocation to become unbalanced from its original levels. Rebalancing is the realignment of your asset categories and styles of your portfolio to their predetermined asset allocation levels. This is necessary to remain consistent with your original objective for your investment portfolio. If, indeed, the selected mutual funds did not perform as expected, adjustments should be made. How is the investment portfolio rebalanced to its original asset allocation? The method that has historically been the most effective in maintaining risk exposure within acceptable limits is described below.

> Those funds that have outperformed the others will be over-weighted. Those that have underperformed will be underweighted. To bring your asset allocation back to its targeted levels, sell those funds that have outperformed the other funds in the portfolio. Acquire more of the lesser performing funds.

If you decide to rebalance your portfolio, the enclosed Rebalancing Worksheet simplifies the process.

Use the Rebalancing Worksheet as follows:

1. Under the heading "Selected Funds," print the names of your selected mutual funds.

2. Under "Asset Allocation Goal …," record the predetermined percentage holdings of each fund.

3. Under "Actual Value," record the actual value for each of your holdings.

4. Under "What Actual Should Be," determine what the actual value for each holding should be. This is done by multiplying each holding's predetermined asset allocation goal by the total value of your account.

5. In the "Variance" column, record the difference. Subtract the actual holding's value from "What Actual Should Be." A positive variance means you own too much of the holding and should sell some of that holding. A negative variance means you own too little and should buy more of that holding.

6. Implement the adjustments. Either contact the custodian of the account or your financial advisor (who should have already notified you of suggested changes) to buy and sell as appropriate.

Asset rebalancing may cause you to owe some taxes. It depends on the type of account that is rebalanced. Any gain from the assets held in an individual account is taxable. (Simply stated, gain is the difference between what you receive less what you paid.) There is no tax consequence on asset sales from a tax-deferred account.

There are two hybrids of the above method. In both instances, you move away from your targeted asset allocation and increase your risk exposure. Even though neither of these methods is recommended, it is important that they are mentioned.

- Do the exact opposite of the recommended method. That is, sell the lesser performing funds to acquire the better performing funds in the attempt to maximize returns. You will also increase your level of risk.

- Let the portfolio drift, and perform no rebalancing.

Rebalancing Worksheet

Category/ Style	Selected Funds	Asset Allocation Goal per Risk Profile Score	Actual Value ($)	What Actual Should Be	Variance
Large Cap Value					
Growth					
Total Large Cap					
Mid-Cap Value					
Growth					
Total Mid-Cap					
Small Cap Value					
Growth					
Total Small Cap					
International					
Fixed					
Total		100%	$	$	$

The recommended approach of selling outperforming funds and buying underperforming funds is consistent with the premise that over the long term, assets will achieve returns comparable to their historic mean or average. (This is called "reversion to the mean.") How often should rebalancing occur? That depends on several factors. One factor is transaction costs. Typically inside a 401(k), 403(b), or similar employee contribution retirement plan, there are no transaction costs to redeem shares of one or more mutual funds and buy shares of other mutual funds. In this case, the frequency of such rebalancing should be quarterly. If, however, your investment portfolio is in a brokerage account, you would incur transaction costs. In this instance a tolerance range should be established. That is, how far should you allow your percentage allocations to drift without adversely affecting your risk tolerance? For example, could you allow your percentage of small caps to increase five percentage points over the target, and your large caps to drop five percentage points below the target and still provide the level of downside risk protection with which you're comfortable? This is only determined through testing and simulations.

Other concerns that could limit your ability to timely rebalance include access to available information and lack of personal time to perform this activity.

REALLOCATING

There are situations and circumstances that necessitate reallocating your portfolio instead of rebalancing. Whereas rebalancing is the process of realigning asset categories and styles of your portfolio to their original targets, reallocation is much more: it's redoing your asset allocation. It's sitting down and redefining your goals and objectives. It's redetermining your tolerance for risk. It's apportioning your investment dollars between stocks and bonds or cash. It's subdividing your stocks among large, mid-, and small cap and international holdings. And it's stylizing your selections between value and growth. Typically, this process is driven by one or more life events that have changed your perspective. Such life events could include marriage, divorce, the birth of a baby, retirement, or the death of a partner.

SUMMARY

Monitoring is the process of tracking something for a special purpose. In this instance, that special purpose is to see how well your portfolio is performing. Monitoring, particularly those statistical factors used to select the mutual funds, is also one way to uncover potential problems. If those measures used to select the mutual funds begin to deteriorate, it may prove necessary to change your selections. However, any changes should only occur after an appropriate amount of time has elapsed and the statistical factors have continued to deteriorate. In the meantime, the best way to maintain the integrity of your asset allocation and correct any imbalances is through rebalancing. The rebalancing technique suggested is selling certain amounts of funds that have outperformed and buying those funds that have not performed as well. If you decide to rebalance, the accompanying worksheet will assist you. If, however, a significant life-changing event has occurred, rebalancing may not be the appropriate tool to adjust your portfolio. It may require reallocation. It may require a complete redetermination of your portfolio. This would consist of:

- Determining portfolio goals and objectives
- Assessing your tolerance for risk

- Reapportioning your investment among stocks and bonds or cash
- Reapportioning among large, mid-, and small cap, and international holdings
- Delineating between value and growth stocks

Chapter 6:

The Mutual Fund Investment Process—A Review

You have just read about an investment process that can help you construct a portfolio of mutual funds. Admittedly, a lot of information was concentrated in those chapters. Because of that, I've summarized the process into useable steps. (At this juncture I'm assuming you either know which mutual funds you will use or are researching ones in specific categories and styles.) Below is a step-by-step review of the overall mutual fund investment process.

1. Go to the library and obtain and familiarize yourself with the appropriate Morningstar Mutual Fund Reports. There is a Morningstar Mutual Fund Report for each category and style of mutual fund, such as large cap value, large cap growth, mid-cap value, etc. For each group, this report offers a large number of funds from which selection data can be drawn.

2. Use the Statistical Analysis Worksheet to record the selection data for each category and style of mutual fund to be examined. That is, large cap value, large cap growth, mid-cap value, mid-cap growth, small cap value, small cap growth, international, and bonds.

3. Evaluate and select those mutual funds that you deem are the most appropriate. Include the determination of the time period to be used: three, five, or ten years.

4. Complete the Risk Profile Questionnaire and determine your risk profile score.

5. Based on your risk profile score, transcribe the fixed component that should be used in your portfolio to Schedule B, Portfolio Construction Worksheet, column D, Revised Allocations on the "Fixed" line.

6. Transcribe your selected mutual funds and the appropriate historic returns and historic standard deviations to Schedule A, Revision to Initial Asset Allocation Worksheet, columns A and C, respectively.

7. Compute the "Weighted Component" historic return and historic standard deviation for each of your mutual funds.

8. Transcribe this information to Schedule B, Portfolio Construction Worksheet, columns A and C.

9. Evaluate the Weighted Results in column C of Schedule B, Portfolio Construction Worksheet.

10. Determine the standard deviation that you're most comfortable with, and record that in column E on the Weighted Results line of Schedule B, Portfolio Construction Worksheet.

11. Revise your Allocations in column D of Schedule B, Portfolio Construction Worksheet, and recompute the revised historic return and standard deviation. (Revisions to your allocations should be based on the Portfolio Construction Assumptions from chapter 4.)

12. Continue the iterations until you've achieved your weighted standard deviation and are comfortable with the related historic return.

13. Monitor, rebalance, or reallocate your portfolio.

Chapter 7:

Conclusion

o o o o o o o o o o o o o o o o o o o o o o o o o o o o o o o o o o o o o o o o o o o o

If you don't know jewelry, know the jeweler.

—*Warren Buffett*
Berkshire Hathaway, Inc.

Whether by design or coincidence, many of us participate in the mutual fund industry. This said, possessing a knowledgeable framework about mutual funds is a crucial component for your overall financial well-being. This understanding can provide the basis from which you can construct and manage your portfolio of mutual funds. Or, you may wish to have this understanding to more effectively deal with other financial professionals, including your financial advisor. *Women & Mutual Fund* provides a platform for you to gain a fundamental knowledge and understanding about mutual funds and the effort it takes to construct and maintain your portfolio of mutual funds.

My purpose was to offer a clear and useable process for selecting mutual funds and to assist you with the allocation and construction of your portfolio and with its continual evaluation. This is a crucial step in your attempt to achieve financial security and independence. You can now take this information and be strong and confident about your knowledge of the mutual fund process and your own portfolio's performance.

Remember: The health of your portfolio is based on continual evaluation and vigilance. I have included for your convenience and further information a Financial Glossary. This includes definitions of terms used in the book and used in the mutual fund industry. It is my hope that *Women & Mutual Funds* assists you in achieving your goals and meets or exceeds your expectations. Let me know. You can send an e-mail to dongudhus@oraclefinancialgroup.com. I'll get back to you. Good luck in your efforts. Because remember, it's your money.

About the Author

Donald S. Gudhus is the founder and president of Oracle Financial Group. Founded in 1993 and located in Center City, Philadelphia, Oracle Financial Group is a Registered Investment Advisor and is a full-service financial advisory firm that specializes in investments, retirement planning, taxes, and insurance protection.

Don has extensive knowledge in investing, having been active in the financial markets, such as the NYSE and the National Association of Securities Dealers Automated Quote System (NASDAQ) before the formation of Oracle. He gained analytical skills as a financial manager with major corporations, such as Conrail, Inc. in Philadelphia and RCA-Hertz Corporation in New York City. This experience honed his ability to quickly identify strategies to solve financial issues.

Don attained his bachelor of business administration degree in finance and economics and master of business administration degree in financial management from Pace University. He is also a graduate of the CFP® Professional Education Program from the College for Financial Planning.

Maintaining his roots in the community is important to Don. One way has been by teaching courses on investing at the Community College of Philadelphia's School for Continuing Education. A dynamic speaker, he also holds seminars for women on a variety of personal financial topics, including retirement planning and investing. Through his cycling efforts, he volunteers with the Multiple Sclerosis Society of the Delaware Valley.

Financial Glossary

Below is a listing of terms that could be heard in any discussion about mutual funds. Some of the terms defined in this section are not used in this book; however, it's important to familiarize yourself with them.

Alpha
: A measure that shows the actual ability of a fund to generate returns that are higher or lower than the fund's expected return given the fund's level of risk as measured by beta. The higher the positive number the better. The higher the negative number the worse.

Asset allocation
: The balancing of an investment portfolio among various categories and styles of stock mutual funds, various types of bond mutual funds, and cash. It is a management tool that seeks to minimize the effects of market volatility by balancing the risks of stocks, bonds, and cash.

Bear market
: A period during which stock prices are declining, such as 2000–02. Most commonly, this market begins at 20 percent from the market's high.

Beta
: Measures the degree of variation or volatility (sometimes called "sensitivity") of a fund's return in relation to a benchmark index, such as the S&P 500, that is considered representative of the market in which the fund is measured. The market index always has a value of 1.00.

Bond

An IOU; a debt instrument. A borrower seeks money from one or more lenders. In return, the borrower agrees to pay the lenders a specified amount of money periodically. At the end of the loan, also called maturity, the borrower pays the lenders the principal amount that was originally borrowed.

Familiar Types of Bonds and Rating Guide
U.S. Treasury

Notes. Intermediate-term (one to nine years) U.S. government IOUs originally issued at face or par value.

Bonds. Long-term (ten or more years) U.S. government IOUs originally issued at face or par value.

Municipal

A tax-exempt IOU issued by a state or local government or a political subdivision. Two types:

General obligation. A bond whose interest payment is backed by the full faith and credit of the issuing entity.

Revenue. A bond whose interest is paid only if the issuer's project earns sufficient income.

Corporate

Mortgage. Issued to purchase specific fixed assets that are then pledged to secure the debt.

Equipment trust. Issued to purchase specific equipment that has substantial resale value and then is pledged as collateral.

Debentures. An unsecured promissory note that is supported by the general creditworthiness of the issuing company.

Convertibles. A debt that can be exchanged for common stock. The conversion is made at a predetermined price.

Zero coupon. A bond that is sold at a discount and where the interest income accrues or accumulates and is not paid until maturity (it is not paid out semiannually or annually).

Junk (high-yield). High-yield bonds are IOUs that are not investment grade. This can cause the investment to be riskier.

Investment grade bonds. AAA (highest S& P) rating, AA, A, and BBB.

Non-investment grade bonds. BB, B CCC, CC, C, D.

Other corporate

Preferred stock. A senior security that usually pays a stated dividend. Although it is not guaranteed, it receives preference over common stock dividends.

Bull market

A period during which stock prices are rising, such as 1995–99. Most commonly that increase begins at 20 percent from the market's low.

Capitalization	The market value of a company that is determined by multiplying the number of common shares of stock outstanding by the market price of a share. Mutual funds are classified according to capitalization (a company's market value) and fall into three categories:
	Large cap. Funds that hold a majority of companies that each have a market value of generally over $10 billion.
	Mid-cap. Funds that hold a majority of companies that each have a market value generally between $2 billion and $10 billion.
	Small cap. Funds that hold a majority of companies that each have a market value of under $2 billion.
Common stock	A security that represents ownership in a corporation; owners are generally called stockholders.
Coupon rate	The stated or specific interest rate attached to a bond.
Dividend	A periodic cash payment from a company's earnings to stockholders; however, this payment may also be made in stock.
Diversification	A strategy used for the deployment of investment dollars among a variety of investment holdings to attempt to optimize returns. It is a systematic way to spread investment dollars to various classes, categories, and styles of investments, such as large cap value, mid-cap growth, small cap value, sectors, individual overseas countries, bonds, and cash, to attempt to achieve the best possible return given a certain level of risk.
Exchange traded funds	Commonly referred to as an ETF, it is a collection of common stocks or bonds that mirror the performance of a market index. ETFs cover all asset classes, such as U.S. large companies, small companies, and overseas companies. Unlike an index mutual fund, these funds can be purchased or sold throughout the trading day. The stocks or bonds that make up the ETF do not change, regardless of how they're performing.

Index mutual funds	A collection of common stocks that mirrors the performance of a market index, such as the S&P 500. There are a limited number of indexes covered. Unlike the ETF, index funds can only be purchased or sold after the close of the trading day. The stocks or bonds that make up the ETF do not change regardless of how they're performing.
Interest	The payment by a borrower to a lender for the use of money.
Maturity	The time a debt becomes due and payable by a borrower.
Mean	The average return (percent) a fund achieves over a specified time. Typically, the shortest relevant time period is one year. Other relevant periods include three, five, and ten years.
Monitoring	The process of periodically reviewing the performance of your portfolio and comparing its asset allocation to your predetermined asset allocation.
Morningstar category	Identifies funds based on the investment holdings in the underlying portfolio.
Mutual fund	An investment vehicle that primarily contains an assortment of stocks (generally common stock) of various corporations and/or bonds issued by federal, state, or local governments or their agencies (Fannie Mae) or various corporations. These holdings are consistent with the fund's objective as outlined in the fund's prospectus. (As with all investments, there is a chance you could loose money. An investment in a mutual fund is not insured or guaranteed by the FDIC or any other governmental agency.)

Stock mutual funds. These are funds whose holdings are usually dominated by the common stock of various companies.

Bond mutual funds. These are funds whose primary (and probably exclusive) holdings are in the debt securities of the U.S. government, its agencies, municipalities, and/or corporations, or foreign governments.

No-load fund. The mutual fund is purchased at net asset value (NAV). There is no upfront or deferred sales commission or fee charged.

Load fund. The purchase of such a mutual fund includes an upfront or deferred sales charge or fee.

• **A shares.** These contain an upfront sales charge that typically ranges from 4.75 percent to 5.75 percent.

• **B shares.** These do not have an upfront sales charge but have a deferred sales charge that typically begins at 5 percent and declines generally over six years. Fund expenses are greater than those of A shares. This share class converts to A shares after typically six years.

• **C shares.** These do not have an upfront sales charge but have a deferred sales charge that typically is 1 percent and lasts for one year. Fund expenses are equivalent to those of B shares. This share class does not convert to A shares.

Types and Styles of Mutual Funds

Money market funds. Contain short-term, high-quality securities that mainly provide safety of principal; the fund's current income is a secondary consideration (includes tax-free funds).

Short and intermediate-term bonds. Contain a mixture of U.S. government securities and creditworthy corporate bonds that usually have an effective maturity and average duration or portfolio life typically from one to ten years.

Long-term bonds. Contain a variety of corporate bonds that emphasize creditworthy companies and usually have an effective maturity greater than ten years. (Average duration or portfolio life could be less than ten years.)

High-yield bonds. Include a range of higher yielding, lower rated corporate bonds (includes tax-free funds).

Balanced funds. Contain a mixture of common stocks and corporate and U.S government bonds. These funds stress both current income and capital appreciation. The equity portion of this type of fund is generally in the large cap category and typically represents the majority of holdings.

Growth funds. Usually contain holdings that possess higher price-to-earnings and price-to-book value ratios in relation to value funds. Fund holdings generally exhibit or are expected to exhibit accelerated earnings and market share growth. (These are generally referred to as companies that are in favor.) Such funds pursue capital appreciation; current income is either not considered or is a secondary issue.

Blend funds. Include a combination of value and growth companies. In this category there are large cap, mid-cap, small cap, and international funds.

Value funds. Typically contain holdings that have lower price-to-earnings and price-to-book value ratios in relation to growth funds. (The calculation of a company's price to earnings ratio is: market price per share/earnings per share.) Fund holdings may include companies that are not followed by the overall market and companies that are in turnaround situations. (These are generally referred to as out-of-favor companies.) Their holdings are generally priced more reasonably and yet show characteristics of performance improvement.

Sector and country funds. Include companies within the same industry or country. For example, energy, technology, biotechnology; China, Japan, Russia.

Domestic funds. Include companies that are primarily in the United States.

International funds. Include companies that are in diverse markets and almost exclusively outside the United States.

Global funds. Include companies in diverse markets, but they can have significant holdings in U.S. companies.

Mutual fund fees and expenses   **Expense ratio.** The management fee paid to the portfolio manager to manage the fund's investments.

12b-1 fee. This is a charge the fund makes for distribution and other related services. It includes fees paid for marketing and selling shares, and advertising, printing, and mailing costs associated with prospectuses and sales literature.

Turnover rate. This shows how quickly the portfolio manager sells existing portfolio holdings and purchases new holdings for the fund managed. Typically, the higher the rate, the higher the transactions costs and the greater the negative impact on a fund's return. This action could cause you to owe taxes.

Front-end load. The fee that is charged the investor for using a broker or investment representative to effect the sale of A shares.

Deferred load. A fee the investor pays only if B or C shares are sold or redeemed prematurely.

Tax cost ratio. Shows the extent to which taxable distributions reduce the mutual fund's return.

Potential capital gain. An estimate of the percent of the mutual fund's assets that came from the increase in value of the stocks in the portfolio.

Net asset value (NAV)	Represents a fund's share price; the price for which one share of a fund may be purchased.
Open-ended investment company	Commonly known as a mutual fund. There is no restriction on the number of shares a fund may sell.
Optimal portfolio	Where the return of the portfolio is the highest achievable given its level of risk.
Price-to-book (P/B) ratio	The price-to-book (value) ratio measures the current premium or discount the market says the company is worth. It is determined by dividing the market price of the stock by its book value.
Price-to-cash-flow (P/CF) ratio	The price-to-cash-flow ratio tells an investor the number of dollars a fund is paying for one dollar of a company's operations or cash flow.
Price-to-earnings (P/E) ratio	The price-to-earnings ratio is the relationship of the price of a share of stock to the firm's per-share earnings. The higher the ratio, the greater the tendency toward a growth orientation. Conversely, the lower the ratio, the greater the tendency toward a value orientation. The higher the P/E, the more the fund is paying for a dollar of earnings. The higher the ratio, the potentially riskier the investment.

Price-to-sales (P/S) ratio	The price-to-sales ratio measures the amount of dollars the fund is paying for a dollar of sales or revenue. The higher the ratio, the potentially riskier the investment.
Percentile rank in category	A measure that shows a mutual fund's rank, in terms of total return, within a particular category and style of investing. This comparison is made against all the other funds that comprise the same category and style of investment.
Potential capital gain	A statistic that provides an estimate of the percent of a mutual fund's assets that are from unrealized capital gains and indicates the potential level of capital gain distribution.
Prospectus	A document that details a mutual fund's investment objectives, related fees and expenses, guidelines to its portfolio's construction, names of the its board of directors, and information about insider holdings.
Principal	The amount of borrowed money owed at maturity; the face amount of the debt.
Reallocating	Redoing your asset allocation. This process is usually driven by one or more life events that have change your perspective. This action can cause you to owe taxes.
Rebalancing	The realignment of your asset categories and styles of your portfolio to their predetermined asset allocation levels. This action can cause you to owe taxes.
Retirement plans (types of)	
	401(k). A retirement savings plan sponsored by an employer. It is funded by employee contributions of pre-tax salary and may have an employer matching contribution. The mutual funds grow tax deferred until they are withdrawn. If the employee changes employer, these 401(k) dollars can be usually transferred to the new employer's plan, withdrawn in a lump-sum or converted to a rollover IRA.
	403(b). A retirement savings plan similar to a 401(k). Unlike a 401(k) that's offered mainly by for-profit corporations, 403(b)'s are offered by not-for-profit organizations, such as universities.

Rollover IRA. A type of IRA that allows an employee leaving an employer to make a lump-sum conversion from his/her qualified plan into an IRA. It maintains the qualified status of the former plan and continues to grow tax-deferred.

Roth IRA. An individual retirement arrangement where contributions are made with after-tax dollars and are never tax deductible. Qualified distributions are tax-free.

SEP-IRA. A simplified employee pension (SEP) plan that allows employers to contribute to IRA retirement accounts maintained by each eligible employee, including owners. The mutual funds grow tax-deferred until withdrawn.

SIMPLE IRA. A savings incentive match plan for employees (SIMPLE) in businesses with less than one hundred employees. Allows employees to contribute pre-tax salary amounts to their mutual funds' account that grows tax-deferred. The employer matches between 2 percent to 3 percent of the employee's contribution.

Traditional IRA. An individual retirement arrangement where contributions are made with after-tax dollars and may be tax deductible. This is dependant on the individual's income. This mutual fund account grows tax-deferred until withdrawn.

R-Squared

Sometimes referred to as the coefficient of determination or R^2. It shows how much of a fund's return can be explained by the fund's "best fit" benchmark index. An R^2 of 100 indicates that the selected market or benchmark index explains all the movements of a fund. The higher the R^2 the more relevant the beta is to the fund's return.

Reversion to the mean

A tendency in the market where assets that achieve above or below average returns will return to their average levels. Unfortunately, you don't know when that will happen.

Risk

The possibility of loss. For the measurement of risk in a mutual fund, there are two generally accepted measurements:

Standard deviation. Measures the difference between the actual returns of a fund (over time) and the average return for that fund over the same time period. It shows how far the actual returns deviate from the average return.

Beta. Measures the degree of variation or volatility (sometimes called sensitivity) of a fund's return in relation to a benchmark index, such as the S&P 500, that is considered representative of the market in which the fund is measured. The benchmark index always has a value of 1.00.

Types of Risk:

Credit risk. An issuer of debt could default on its obligation to pay principal and interest; a rating company could downgrade the credit rating of the issuer.

Foreign risk. A company's value could decline because of political instability, inaccurate information about foreign issuers, government actions or currency exchange rates.

Inflation risk. A rise in consumer prices will erode the purchasing power of the U.S. dollar. (One dollar buys less, or it costs more dollars to buy the same item.)

Interest rate risk. If interest rates go up, bond and other income-oriented security prices go down.

Liquidity and Valuation risk. Securities that were liquid when purchased could become illiquid or hard to value.

Market risk. Investments that move in unison with the overall market, as measured by r-squared and beta.

Small company risk. These securities may have greater risk than large companies and may be more volatile.

Style risk. At any time, the market could favor growth stocks over value stocks and vice versa at particular capitalization levels.

Risk-free rate	The current yield of a three-month treasury bill.
Risk Profile Questionnaire	A series of questions regarding your investment preferences, likes, and dislikes. Its aim is to gauge your tolerance for risk.

Section 529 college savings plans	A tax-advantaged investment plan designed to encourage savings for future higher education expenses of a designated beneficiary. There are two types of plans: prepaid and savings. Prepaid plans allow you to purchase tuition credits at today's rates for future use. Savings plans are based on performance of the selected investments, typically mutual funds. Prepaid plans are sponsored by states or higher education institutions. Savings plans are only sponsored by states.
Sharpe ratio	A measure that shows whether and to what extent a mutual fund earns a return that is in excess of the return it was expected to achieve given the riskiness of the investment.
Standard deviation	Measures the difference between the actual returns of a fund (over time) and the average return for that fund over the same time. It shows how far the actual returns deviate from the average return. Risk is measured by standard deviation. The higher the ratio the better.
Stewardship grade	Morningstar provides an overall assessment of the manner in which the mutual fund is run; the degree to which the interests of management, the board of directors, and investors are aligned; and the protection of shareholder interests from potential conflicting interests of management. The determination of a fund's grade is separate from the manner in which Morningstar rates the performance of the fund. The criteria used to establish an overall alphabetic grade for stewardship includes: (1) the manner in which regulatory issues are handled; (2) the quality of the fund's board of directors; (3) the level of incentives given to the managers; (4) the fees charged investors; and (5) the fund's corporate culture. Each component can receive a grade as high as 2 and as low as 0. (Regulatory issues can receive a grade as low as—2.) The sum of the five components yields the stewardship grade: 9–10 points = A; 7–8.5 points = B; 5–6.5 points = C; 3–4.5 points = D; 2.5 points or lower = F.
Tax-cost ratio	A statistic that shows the extent to which taxable distributions reduce the mutual fund's return.

Tenure   The time spent by the fund manager on managing, directing, and
                                implementing the strategies and investments of the managed
                                fund.

Total assets   The amount of money a fund has under management. This is
                                oftentimes called net assets.

Yield   Annual interest paid by a bond issuer divided by the market value
                                of that bond.

References

"Asset Allocation: Revisiting the Debate." Morningstar, February 27, 1997.

Baron Partners Fund. Morningstar Report, December 31, 2006. (Reprinted by permission.)

Beebower, Gilbert, Michael Hogan, and Robert Ludwig. "Asset Allocation: Is It a Hoax?" *SEI*, Spring 1998.

Brinson, Gary P., Randolph Hood, and Gilbert Beebower. "Determinants of Portfolio Performance." *Financial Analysts Journal*, July/August 1986.

Brinson, Gary P., Brian D. Singer, and Gilbert Beebower. "Determinants of Portfolio Performance II: An Update." *Financial Analysts Journal*, May/June 1991.

Callan Associates. The Periodic Table of Investment Returns, 1987–2006.

Darst, David M. *The Art of Asset Allocation*. New York: McGraw-Hill Companies, 2003.

Evensky, Harold. "The Hoax is a Hoax." *Financial Planning*, November 1997.

Russell Investments. "Annual percentage returns for large and mid-cap companies, growth and value indices," 1994–2003.

Jahnke, William. "The Asset Allocation Hoax." *Journal of Financial Planning*, February 1997.

Ibbotson, Roger G. *Stocks, Bonds, Bills, and Inflation 2006 Yearbook: Valuation Edition*. Chicago: Ibbotson Associates, 2006.

Ibbotson, Roger G., and Paul D. Kaplan. "Does Asset Allocation Policy Explain 40, 90, or 100 Percent of Performance?" Available at www.ibbotson.com/research, December 1998, revised April 1999.

Morningstar, Inc. Licensed reprint of *Baron Partners Fund*, 2006.

Morningstar Principia Mutual Funds. CD-ROM, March 2006.

Risk Profile Questionnaire. H. D. Vest Investment Services, Inc. 2004.

Singer, Brian. "Hoax and Strawmen." *Journal of Financial Planning*, October 1997.

Statman, Meir. "The Numbers Racket Rages On." *Financial Planning*, April 1998.

Study Guide, CFP III: Investment Planning. College for Financial Planning, May 1991.

Webster's Third New International Dictionary. Springield, MA: Merriam-Webster, Inc., 1993.

Wikipedia, The Free Encyclopedia. Available online at www.wikipedia.org.

Wilson, Philip. "Mad as Hell." *Dow Jones Investment Advisor*, February 1998.

Index

A

A shares, 6, 58
alpha statistic, 16–17, 53
asset allocation. *See also* diversification;
  monitoring; portfolio construction
    example of, 23
    importance of, 23–26
    initial, 34–35
    in mutual funds, 5
    overview, 22–23, 28, 47–48, 53
    reallocating, 45, 48, 61
    rebalancing, 42–45, 48, 61

B

B shares, 6, 58
balanced funds, 4, 58
bear market, 53
Beebower, Gilbert L., 24
beta statistics, 15–16, 53, 63
blend funds, 2, 4, 59
bond mutual funds, 2–3, 32, 57
bonds, 27, 54–55, 58
Brinson, Gary P., 24
bull market, 55

C

C shares, 6, 58
Callan Periodic Table of Investment Returns, 25
capital gains, potential, 19, 60, 61
capitalization, 1–2, 56
categories, of funds, 1. *See also* capitalization
coefficient of determination, 15–16, 62
college savings plans, 64
common stock, 1, 56
contingent deferred sales charges, 6–7
corporate bonds, 54–55
cost, of initial investment, 6
country funds, 4, 59
coupon rate, 56
credit quality, 3
credit ratings, 3, 55
credit risk, 63

D

deferred loads, 18–19, 60
diversification, 5, 56. *See also* asset allocation
dividend, 56
domestic funds, 4, 59

E

equity market, investment in, xii–xiv
exchange traded funds (ETFs), 5, 56
expense ratio, 17, 59
expenses. *See* fees and expenses

F

fees and expenses
  and mutual fund selection, 17–19
  monitoring of, 42
  transaction costs, 6, 44–45
  types of, 6–7, 59–60
foreign risk, 63
401 (k) accounts, 10, 61
403 (b) accounts, 10, 61
front-end loads, 18, 60
funds. *See* mutual funds

G

gains. *See* returns
global funds, 4, 59
goals
  and mutual fund selection, 20–21
  overview, xii–xiv,
  qualitative measures, 9–10
  reallocating and, 45
  rebalancing and, 42–45
  risk profile and, 26–27, 29–30
growth funds, 2, 4, 32–34, 59
Gudhus, Donald S., xiv–xv

H

high-yield bonds, 3, 58
historic information, 37–39, 41–42
Hood, Randolph, 24

I

index mutual funds, 5, 57
individual IRAs, 62
inflation risk, 63
initial asset allocation, 34–35
interest, 57, 65
interest rate risk, 63
intermediate-term bonds, xii–xiv, 3, 58
international funds, 4, 32–34, 59
investment goals. *See* goals
investment grade bonds, 55
investment, initial, 6
investment styles, 1–2
IRAs, xii, 8–9, 10, 19, 61–62

J

Jahnke, William, 25

L

large cap funds, 2, 32–34
large company stocks, xii–xiv, 32
liquidity risk, 63
load funds, 6, 18–19, 58. *See also* no-load funds
long-term bonds, xii–xiv, 3, 58
lower range, of standard deviation, 15

M

management fees, 6–7
managers. *See* portfolio managers
market risk, 63
maturity, 57
mean
    defined, 57
    reversion to, 44, 62
mid-cap funds, 2, 32–34
money market funds, 3, 58
monitoring
    defined, 57
    as part of investment process, 42, 48, 50
    reallocating, 45, 48, 61
    reasons for, 21, 41–42, 45–46
    rebalancing, 42–45, 48, 61
Morningstar
    categories, 57
    reports, 9, 13, 35, 47
    stewardship grade, 10, 64

municipal bonds, 3, 54
mutual funds
    defined, 57
    analysis of, 9–19
    benefits of, 5–6
    fees and expenses of, 6–7
    outperforming and underperforming, 42–45
    overview, xi–xii, 47–48, 57–58
    selection of, 8–9, 20–21, 32–33
    stock, 1–2
    types of, 3–5, 58–59

N

net asset value (NAV), 60
no-load funds, 6, 18, 57. *See also* load funds
non-investment grade bonds, 55
nontaxable accounts, 19

O

open-ended investment companies, 60
optimal portfolios, 31–32, 60
Oracle Financial Group, xv, 51
outperforming funds, 42–45

P

percentile rankings, 11–13, 61
performance. *See* returns
portfolio construction. *See also* asset allocation;
  portfolios
    adjustments in, 36, 39
    assumptions for, 32–34
    initial asset allocation, 34–35
    overview, 31–32, 39–40, 47–48
    worksheets, 37, 38
portfolio managers, 5, 14, 21
portfolios. *See also* monitoring; portfolio
  construction
    optimal, 31–32, 60
    performance studies of, 24–26
potential capital gain, 19, 21, 60, 61
price-to-book (P/B) ratio, 60
price-to-cash-flow (P/CF) ratio, 60
price-to-earnings (P/E) ratio, 60
price-to-sales (P/S) ratio, 61
principal, 61
prospectus, 61

Q

qualitative measures, for mutual fund selection, 9–10
questionnaire, risk profile, 26–27, 29–30, 63

R

ranges, of standard deviation, 15
rankings, percentile, 11, 13, 61
reallocating, 45, 48, 61
rebalancing, 42–45, 48, 61
retirement plans, 8–9, 10, 19, 61–62
returns
    documents regarding, 25. *See also* Morningstar
    examples, by investment type, xii–xiv
    measures of, 14–15, 16–17
    in portfolio construction, 39
    studies regarding, 24–26
reversion to the mean, 44, 62
Revision to Initial Asset Allocation Worksheet, 35, 37
risk
    control of, 23–26
    defined, 62
    measures of, 14–16, 16–17, 62–63
    monitoring and, 42
    reallocating and, 45
    types of, 63
risk profile
    and allocation of assets, 35, 39
    questionnaire, 26–27, 29–30, 63
    and selection of assets, 20–21, 31–34
risk tolerance. *See* risk profile
risk-free rates, 63
rollover IRAs, 10, 62
Roth IRAs, 62
r-squared. *See* r2 statistic
r2 statistic, 15–16, 62
Rule 12b-1 fees, 6–7, 59

S

sales charge, 6
Section 529 college savings plans, 64
sector funds, 4, 59
selection, of mutual funds
    overview, 8–9, 20–21, 47–48
    qualitative measures, 9–10

statistical factors, 10–19
SEP-IRA, 62
Sharpe ratio, 17, 64
short-term bonds, 3, 58
SIMPLE IRAs, 62
Singer, Brian D., 24
small cap funds, 2, 32–34
small company risk, 63
small company stocks, xii–xiv
standard deviation. *See also* risk; risk profile
    calculation of, 14–15
    defined, 63, 64
    in portfolio construction, 21, 27, 35–36, 39–40, 48
    and risk assessment, 17
Statistical Analysis Worksheet, 12
statistical factors. *See also* standard deviation
    alpha, 16
    beta, 15–16
    fees and expenses and, 17–19
    for mutual fund selection, 10–19
    overview, 21
    percentile rankings, 11, 61
    Sharpe ratio, 17, 64
    standard deviation, 14–15
    summary, 20–21
    tenure and, 14
    time periods in, 11, 14, 35, 47, 57, 63
stewardship grade, 64
stock market, investment in, xii–xiv
stock mutual funds, 1–2, 27, 32, 57
style risk, 63

T

tax cost ratio, 19, 60, 64
taxes, 19, 43
tenure, 14, 65
time periods
    historic information, 39, 41–42
    life span, for investments, 11
    in statistical analysis, 11, 14, 35, 47, 57, 63
tolerance, for risk. *See* risk profile
total assets, 65
transaction costs, 6, 44–45
Treasury bills, xii–xiv
Treasury bonds, xii–xiv, 54

Treasury notes, 54
turnover ratio, 18, 60
12b-1 fees, 6–7, 18, 59

U
underperforming funds, 42–45
upper range, of standard deviation, 15

V
valuation risk, 63
value funds, 2, 4, 32–34, 59
volatility, 15

W
worksheets
    Portfolio Construction, 36, 38, 39
    Rebalancing, 44
    Revision to Initial Asset Allocation, 35, 37
    Risk Profile Questionnaire, 26–27, 29–30, 63
    Statistical Analysis, 12

Y
yield, 65